EUCHARISTIC SOUNDINGS

General Editors
✠ Maurice Couve de Murville, Archbishop of Birmingham
Fr David McLoughlin
Fr David Evans

Oscott College was founded near Birmingham in 1794 at a time when students and staff from the English Catholic colleges abroad were being driven home by the French Revolution. In 1838 it occupied new buildings at Sutton Coldfield, built in the Gothic style, in a move which inaugurated an ambitious phase of the Catholic Revival in England. Oscott is the seminary of the Archdiocese of Birmingham which also has students from many other dioceses.

The Oscott series aims at continuing the role of Oscott as an intellectual and spiritual centre of English Catholicism for close on two hundred years.

Other titles in the series are:

Owen F. Cummings

EUCHARISTIC SOUNDINGS

Oscott Series 10

VERITAS

First published 1999 by
Veritas Publications
7-8 Lower Abbey Street
Dublin 1

Copyright © Owen F. Cummings 1999

ISBN 1 85390 487 2

Coláiste
Mhuire gan Smal
Luimneach

Class 234.163
Suffix CUM
ACC U132 6515

MIC0003866
WITHDRAWN
MIC LIBRARY

British Library Cataloguing
in Publication Data.
A catalogue record for
this book is available
from the British Library.

The author and publishers are grateful to the Editors of
Emmanuel, *The Clergy Review*, *One in Christ* and *Priests and
People* for permission to reproduce material published in these
journals.

Cover Illustration: Octateuch Scene, Or. 481 Folio 105v, by
permission of the British Library
Cover design by Bill Bolger
Printed in the Republic of Ireland by Betaprint Ltd, Dublin

CONTENTS

To Cathy, companion of twenty-five years, with gratitude.

FOREWORD

The Eucharist has been described in a great variety of theological images. These include the Eucharist as the sacrament of Christ in the world, the memorial of the sacrificial death and resurrection of Christ, the source and means of unity, food for the journey, bread broken for a new world, the place where the dead are remembered and the communion of saints celebrated, the assembly of Christians who worship the Triune God, a pledge of future glory and a foretaste of life to come. The Eucharist also keeps alive the liberating, healing and prophetic memory of Christ in the world. Consequently it is often said by way of summary that the Eucharist is the source and summit of the Church's life.

There can be little doubt historically speaking that it is the Eucharist which has held together the Catholic Church down through the centuries and also many of the other Christian Churches since the time of the Reformation. And yet there is division among the Churches in their understanding of the Eucharist. In spite of this painful division some very significant agreed statements on the Eucharist have been issued in recent times. These statements include, for example, *Eucharistic Doctrine,* issued in 1971 by the Anglican Roman Catholic International Commission, and the Lima document *Baptism, Eucharist and Ministry,* produced in 1982 by the Faith and Order Commission of the World Council of Churches. These two documents and indeed others represent real signs of hope for the ecumenical movement.

The recent teaching document on the Eucharist and norms for sacramental sharing entitled *One Bread, One Body,* published in 1998 by the Catholic Bishops' Conferences of England and Wales, Ireland and Scotland, generated a lot of interest and not a little controversy, especially in Ireland. Some were dismayed by the intensity of the theological exchanges in the national news media and religious journals such as *The Furrow, Doctrine and Life* and *The Tablet.* Heated controversy can be a sign of the vitality of faith. However, if the issues are left without further clarification there is the possibility that the controversy may not have have been as fruitful as it could have been.

Eucharistic Soundings was written prior to the publication of *One Bread, One Body* and therefore does not have this document in mind as such. However, this particular fact makes *Eucharistic Soundings* all the more valuable and interesting. This new book offers a series of essays on the Eucharist which is useful background to this recent controversy and in many respects is complementary to the questions addressed in *One Bread, One Body. Eucharistic Soundings* is also an important contribution in itself to ecumenical dialogue and ongoing theological debate about the Eucharist.

From an ecumenical point of view Cummings has two very important essays. In chapter 3, entitled 'The Reformers on Eucharistic Theology', he shows that there are elements of a eucharistic ecclesiology in Luther, Zwingli and Calvin. The axiom that 'the Eucharist makes the Church' is not absent from the classical reformers. In chapter 9 Cummings shows that John Macquarrie as an Anglican articulates a theology of the Eucharist that is indistinguishable from the Roman Catholic understanding of the Eucharist.

At the theological level there are important clarifications and expositions of doctrine. Cummings shows, for example, how it is possible to have an understanding of the Eucharist that does not depend on Hellenistic metaphysics (Chapter 1). Likewise in 'Medieval Eucharistic Theology' (Chapter 2), he indicates that a perfectly orthodox theology of Eucharist existed prior to the language of transubstantiation. In this way *Eucharistic Soundings* illustrates in different chapters the existence of a plurality of views on the Eucharist within an underlying unity of faith.

In chapters 4 to 6 he outlines modern developments within Catholic Eucharistic theology from Pius X to Pope John Paul II. In chapter 7 on 'The Eucharistic presence of Christ' he emphasises the many presences of Christ found in the teaching of Vatican II and Pope Paul VI's encyclical *Mysterium Fidei*. In chapter 8 Cummings spells out the social implications of the Eucharist in a way that highlights how important it is to resist the privatisation of eucharistic faith.

In chapter 10, 'Liturgy and the Parish', he seeks to avoid the extremes represented by those requesting Latin Masses and, on the other hand, those who encourage freewheeling, presidential entreupreneurism.

These essays are marked by a keen sense of historical development in eucharistic theology. Cummings is a reliable guide to the Catholic theology of the Eucharist: balanced in his judgements, informed in his reading of the tradition, liturgically aware, ecumenically sensitive, and theologically accurate. *Eucharistic Soundings* is a welcome and timely publication that will enrich the perspectives of *One Bread, One Body* and, at the same time, advance theological understanding of the Eucharist.

Dermot A Lane
Mater Dei Institute of Education, Dublin 3

1

CYPRIAN OF CARTHAGE AND EPHREM OF NISIBIS: TWO PATRISTIC APPROACHES TO THE EUCHARIST

Introduction

Some markers have been laid down recently about the nature of theology and of theological education, indicating that the Church is not being as well served at this time as it might be. One thinks, for example, of Thomas C. Oden's recent book, *Requiem*, which is a post-liberal critique of the mainline, liberal, ecclesiastical establishment, with particular reference to theological education.[1] Oden's central thesis has to do with seminaries and institutes of theological education in the Reformed tradition – although he notes that his critique is pertinent also to some Catholic institutions – and is best summarised in his own words:

> ...The Church that weds itself to modernity is already a widow within postmodernity... the *theos* in 'theo-logy' for three decades has come to mean anything. You will fill in the blanks. You can name whatever you are doing theology, and no one will stop to ask why.[2]

Even if it is conceded that there may be some degree of caricature in Oden's analysis of the contemporary theological-educational scene, there is much with which to identify, and not only within the halls of the theological academy. One could find examples of catechesis and preaching that are infected with the decadent modernity described by Oden. Oden's alternative to the liberal programme that seeks 'confirmation from the culture' is a spiritual and theological formation 'by the apostolic tradition, as seen through varied refractions of historical memory'.[3] There is no adequate substitute for an immersion in the pluriform and rich Christian tradition as preparation for ministry in the Church at whatever level. This essay, outlining two patristic approaches to the Eucharist, is *one* refraction of historical memory. My hope is to explore something of the historical diversity of patristic Christianity in North Africa and Syria by giving particular attention to the Eucharist from their somewhat different cultural and theological perspectives. Cyprian of Carthage and Ephrem of Nisibis are taken as representatives of these two Christianities. Having described something of their respective approaches, the last part of the essay will attempt to relate the Cyprianic and Ephremite styles of Christianity to the Church today.

Cyprian of Carthage

The origins of Christianity in North Africa are unknown. The earliest evidence of the existence of the Church in the region is the martyrdom of twelve men and women from Scillium in Numidia in 180 CE. The language of the African Church was Latin – Africa had a Latin Bible before Rome, and can justly be described as the homeland of Christian Latin literature. There has, however, been modest speculation about the origins of the Church in Carthage. The old city of Carthage, the arch-enemy of Rome, was destroyed in 149 BCE, but was re-founded by Julius Caesar in 44 BCE. Veteran soldiers were sent out at colonists.[4] In the writings of the African Church there is present a strong military element, found especially in Tertullian and Cyprian. At the same time, there is considerable use of legal language. Such observations have led some to believe that the African Church had been singularly influenced by the Roman military, perhaps even owing its origins to converted soldiers.[5]

Whether, in fact, this is the case or not, there is no mistaking the disciplinary and military emphasis in Cyprian. During the eighteen months of peace he experienced as the new bishop of Carthage, his watchword was 'discipline'. He described his episcopate as 'serving discipline in peace'.[6] For Cyprian, the Church must be trained in all its ranks like an army, and obedience is the clear presupposition of such training. Peter Hinchliff writes:

> Disobedience was a sin about which [Cyprian] used the strongest possible language and, as a bishop, he did not hesitate to claim that he ought to be obeyed.[7]

In terms of religion, probably much of the ancient Punic religion of Carthage lived on, even among the Christian population, betraying some of the following elements: terror and awe in the face of the gods; a tradition of rigorism and fanaticism; the eulogy of martyrdom. Certainly, the African Church laid stress on the strictness of moral discipline, and the expectation was that no attempt should be made to escape from martyrdom.[8]

The first African Church Father writing in Latin was Tertullian (c. 160-220 CE). There is little or no evidence that Cyprian used or read any other theologian. When asking for the works of Tertullian, Cyprian would say to his secretary, '*Da magistrum*', 'Hand me the master'.[9] This was, however, no slavish dependence, because Cyprian was well able to distance himself from positions of Tertullian when he judged the situation to warrant it.[10] The great authority was Holy Scripture, and in his first few months as a Christian, he produced three volumes of *Testimonies,* collections of scriptural proof-texts.

The earliest biographical account of Cyprian comes from his deacon, Pontius. He began with Cyprian's conversion and birth into the Church, and not with his biological birth.[11] Cyprian's life as a Christian was very short – about twelve years (246-258 CE). He was thoroughly trained in rhetoric, and had a broad literary education. Unlike other North African writers, he avoids altogether quotations from pagan authors. It is as though his baptism and initiation into the Christian faith required putting all that behind him. He was also a man of considerable wealth. He gave away in alms and charity a great deal of his riches. In both of these ways he signalled an absolute break with his former way of life.[12]

The Church had not suffered serious persecution for a long period of time, and in Cyprian's estimation this period of peace had led to laxity in almost every area of the Church's life. In his treatise, *On the Lapsed,* he wrote:

> There is no religious zeal left among the priests, no unalloyed faith in the ministries, no compassion in works, no moral discipline.[13]

Again, describing the Church in a letter, he commented:

> Everyone knows how virgins consecrated to the Lord have taken to sleeping with men, and that one of the latter is a deacon.[14]

The peace was not to last during Cyprian's episcopate. Decius, Roman Emperor from 249-251 CE, undertook the first systematic persecution of Christians, beginning with the execution of Fabian, Bishop of Rome, in January 250 CE. By June of the same year, all citizens were required to provide proof or verification of having offered sacrifice to the emperor. Many Christians gave way. In Carthage, the Roman magistrates who were issuing the certificates verifying that the bearer had offered sacrifice in accordance with the imperial decree, could not cope with the crowds.

The widespread apostasy left Cyprian with an enormous pastoral problem: how to cope with the lapsed, with those who had apostasised, when the persecution came to an end. To grasp something of Cyprian's predicament, one must call to mind that the rigorous discipline of public penance, the *exomologesis,* was at this time securely in place for the sins of adultery, murder and apostasy. Should those who had sacrificed, and, therefore, technically had apostasised, be required to undergo the process of public penance? Should those who had not actually sacrificed, but who had received through bribery a certificate verifying that they had sacrificed, also be cut off from communion until they had performed public penance? The pastoral issue was exacerbated by the strong expectation in North Africa that one should be prepared to die for one's faith.[15] Two further complications enter the scene. First, Cyprian himself left the city when the persecution began. It is likely that he was convinced that the Church in Carthage would survive only if he remained to guide it with a firm supportive hand at this time of crisis. Clearly, however, his action was open to other, negative interpretations, and his opponents were not slow to take them up.[16] Secondly, some of the clergy in Carthage were permitting the lapsed to return to the Eucharist without the due process of public penance. In part, this was in response to the request of confessors – those who had acknowledged their Christian faith but had not been martyred – that some of the lapsed be restored to communion when the persecution had ended, and the bishop and the clergy had been able to meet on the matter. Cyprian insisted that all normal cases of lapsation should wait until peace came, but he recognised also certain extenuating circumstances in which reconciliation with the Church could be effected through the recommendation of a confessor and the imposition of hands by a presbyter.[17]

Despite his difficulties in dealing with the situation, and his firm insistence on obedience to the bishop, Cyprian never adopts the position of his 'master', Tertullian. He never says that the lapsed are beyond forgiveness. Throughout his entire episcopate, and especially during times of turmoil and conflict, Cyprian's overwhelming interest was in maintaining the unity of the Church. As well as the Decian persecution, he had to deal also with internal threats to the unity of the Church from the very beginning – issues of authority, discipline, obedience. Peter Hinchliff sums up these threats as follows:

> The nature of a bishop's authority, his relationship with his own people and with other bishops, the meaning of baptism, the sinfulness of schism, the firm boundaries of the Church, all are bound up with [the question] of unity.[18]

Cyprian's basic position on unity, authority and the bishop is this: the bishop is the source of unity in his own diocese; all authority stems from him; the unity of the Church as a whole springs from the common action of the bishops. Thus, in his letters we find him writing as if he were able to say with precision just who was in the Church and who was not. 'He believed that the Holy Spirit was in the Church empowering the ministers: those who are outside of the Church cannot give the Holy Spirit for they do not possess him.'[19] There is no confusion or combat between order and spirit for Cyprian, between what might be called today the institutional Church and charismatic Christianity.[20]

Cyprian, the Eucharist and Letter 63

Cyprian's churchmanship was thoroughly institutional in the best sense of that term. His theology was also profoundly eucharistic, as has been well established by John D. Laurance.[21] To get a flavour of Cyprian's eucharistic thinking, one could not do better than to examine one of his letters, Letter 63, which has been described as 'the only ante-Nicene writing that deals exclusively with celebration of the Eucharist.'[22] The letter was written probably between 254 and 256 CE, some time after the Decian persecution had come to an end.[23] It is addressed to a brother bishop, Caecilius – though from remarks in 1:2 it seems more to have been dedicated to him than addressed to him – and it reflects on difficulties concerning 'the Lord's cup'. The major difficulty is that some Christians are using water only in the eucharistic cup and not wine (2:1). Wine, maintains Cyprian, cannot be omitted because 'wine signifies the blood of Christ' (2:12), and he goes on to conduct a typological and allegorical defence of the use of wine, using Old Testament texts (Gn 9:20ff; 14:18ff; 49:8ff; Pr 9:1ff; Is 63:2). On the other hand, whenever water is mentioned in Scripture, it is an allusion to baptism, and it would seem that Cyprian is tackling proof-texts used by the Aquarians concerning water.[24] On the basis of the Lord's words at the last Supper – 'I shall not drink further of this fruit of the vine, until that day when I shall drink with you new wine in the kingdom of my Father' – Cyprian takes it as axiomatic that 'if there is no wine in the cup... the Lord's sacrifice is not duly consecrated and celebrated' (9:3).

Next, Cyprian introduces an interesting argument from the experience of drinking wine. Drinking wine relaxes people, enabling them to forget their troubles and woes. Drinking the blood of Christ enables Christians to forget their former worldly ways, and to become joyful in the way of the Lord (11:3). Holy Scripture endorses this because the Holy Spirit alludes to the Lord's cup in Psalm 22:5: 'Your cup which intoxicates is truly excellent'. Since no one can become intoxicated with water, the Lord's cup must be mixed with wine (11:2). Mixing wine with water in the celebration of the Eucharist enables Cyprian to reach a profound ecclesiological conclusion: 'When, therefore, wine is mixed with water in the cup, the people are made one with Christ and the multitude of believers are bonded and united with him in whom they have come to believe. And this bonding and union between water and wine in the Lord's cup is achieved in such a way that nothing thereafter can separate their intermingling' (13:1-2). The union suggests yet another and related image for Cyprian: '...for just as numerous grains are gathered, ground and mixed all together to make into one loaf of bread, so in Christ, who is the bread of heaven, we know there is but one body and that every one of us has been fused together and made one with it' (13:4).

If we follow the Lord's own words in the gospel, if Christ alone is to be heeded, then 'we must make no fundamental change to what has been divinely instituted, relying on some man-made tradition' (14:3). In this fashion, just as Christ is himself the High Priest of the Father who offered himself in sacrifice to the Father, so the priest 'offers up a true and complete sacrifice to God the Father in the Church when he proceeds to offer it just as he sees Christ himself to have offered it' (14:4).

Cyprian now comes to what may have been one of the motives for not using wine in the Eucharist: 'It may be that some feel apprehensive at our morning sacrifices that if they taste wine they may exhale the smell of the blood of Christ' (15:2). Drinking wine so early in the morning means that they run the risk of being discovered as Christians with all the possible penalties of that discovery. Cyprian links this kind of thinking to a refusal to remain steadfast in time of persecution: 'That is the sort of thinking which causes our brethren to become reluctant to share even in Christ's sufferings in times of persecution by being ashamed of the blood that Christ shed himself' (15:2).

One of the strongest expressions of the sacrificial dimensions of the Eucharist occurs in this letter of Cyprian's. 'Because at every sacrifice we offer we mention the passion of our Lord… indeed, the passion of our Lord is the sacrifice we offer… then we should follow exactly what the Lord did' (17:1). Although Cyprian's language is very strong and precise in this passage about eucharistic sacrifice – 'the passion of our Lord *is* the sacrifice we offer' – he does not appear to be introducing a novel idea. Rather, the Eucharist as sacrifice is known by Cyprian, but is expressed by him in such a clear fashion as to appeal to later generations of Christian thinkers. Dom Gregory Dix puts it like this: 'His explanation of the sacrifice has a simplicity which recommended it to popular devotional thought, and the sort of logical directness and unity which has always appealed to Western theologians'.[25] It is very likely that Cyprian's resolute insistence on the sacrificial dimension of the Eucharist in this letter and elsewhere also has to do with the fact that martyrs in the Christian community at Carthage were performing in their own lives the passion of Christ, sacrificing their own lives for the love of him whose body they were. 'In Cyprian's thinking, by celebrating the Eucharist, partaking of the body of Christ, and sharing his cup, we learn to become ourselves a Eucharist, that is, an offering or sacrifice. We become this in everyday Christian life by acts of charity that express our unremitting concern for our brethren, but also and especially by the total gift of self in the act of martyrdom which configures the Christian to the sacrifice of Christ.'[26] Cyprian himself joined the glorious band of martyrs, totally conformed to the sacrifice of Christ, in mid-September, 258 CE.[27]

Ephrem of Nisibis

In coming to Ephrem of Nisibis, we move not only from Christianity in North Africa to Christianity in Syria, but also from Latin to Syriac. Syriac as a language is a branch of Aramaic, and was spoken in and around Edessa from shortly before the beginning of Christianity. Active Christians in the area led to its extensive use in the early Church. One of the outstanding literary genres in Syriac is liturgical poetry of which Ephrem is the best example. Until about 400 CE Syriac Christianity was at its most Semitic in character, not greatly influenced by Hellenistic thought patterns.[28]

According to Syriac sources, Ephrem (c. 306-373 CE) was the son of a pagan priest at Nisibis, his home town, but most scholars today believe that there is enough evidence from his own writings that his parents were Christian. He was ordained a deacon, probably by Bishop James of Nisibis. After the cession of Nisibis to Persia in 363 CE, Ephrem went to live, along with most of the

Nisibene Christian community, in Edessa, which was in the Roman Empire and was, therefore, a place of safety for Christians, and this is where most of his extant works were written. Ephrem wrote mainly in verse. One scholar insists that Ephrem's Syriac verse is so involved and intricate that it 'will not translate without a host of explanatory notes' and that 'the only way to study Ephrem properly is in Syriac'.[29] While that is unquestionably desirable, we are none the less well served by contemporary translators of Ephrem, especially by Sebastian Brock and Kathleen McVey, and references to their translations will be made throughout this essay. As a Church father, Ephrem is much less well known than others, including Cyprian. There are at least two reasons for this. First, the fact that he wrote in Syriac makes him so much less accessible to Western readers and students unacquainted with the language, but in no way does this mean that Ephrem and his Syriac-writing colleagues are less valuable in Christian theology. Sebastian Brock writes:

> If these oriental fathers are very little known to Western Christians, this is due, not to any intrinsic inferiority on their part, but to the heavily Eurocentric character of the academic study of Church history and doctrine.[30]

Second, the fact that Ephrem was essentially a poet renders him somewhat suspect, even though he was 'the greatest poet of the patristic age, and perhaps the only theologian-poet to rank beside Dante'.[31] Western analytic and systematic thinkers have not tended to take with great seriousness those whose theological vision is mediated through poetry.[32]

A major and perduring theme in Ephrem's theological poetry is the inaccessibility of the divine to human reason. That God exists is knowable, but the nature of God remains impenetrable to human intelligence:

> …Thousand thousands stand, and ten thousand
> thousands haste.
> The thousands and ten thousands cannot search
> out the One:
> for all of them stand, in silence and serve.
> He has no heir of his throne, save the Son who
> is of him.
> In the midst of silence is the enquiry into him,
> when the watchers [i.e. angels] come to search
> him out.
> They attain to silence and are stayed.[33]

Only the Son can comprehend the Father because they are of the same nature. It is not, however, the case that while God remains opaque to our human intelligence and enquiry, we on the other hand are quite transparent to ourselves. If we are mysteries to ourselves, *a fortiori,* God is mysterious to us:

> If then our knowledge cannot even achieve a knowledge of itself, how does it dare investigate the birth of him who knows all things? How can the servant, who does not properly know himself, pry into the nature of his master?[34]

Interestingly, Ephrem describes the Arians as rationalistic, and as the ones who 'scrutinise', because of their basic implication that they 'know' the nature of God.[35] This attempt to penetrate and even to exhaust the mystery of God is condemned also when it impacts other 'mysteries'. For example, Ephrem is just as deeply opposed to any effort to grasp comprehensively the meaning of the Eucharist:

> Our Lord has become our living bread, and we shall delight in our new cup. Come, let us then eat it without investigation, and without scrutiny let us drink his cup.

> Who disdains blessings and fruits and sits down to
> investigate their nature? A human being needs to live.
> Come, let us live and not die in the depth of investigation.[36]

Undoubtedly, this theme of Ephrem's finds at least some of its roots
in the notion of God in the Old Testament. One thinks of those
passages where God's nature remains unknowable and even hidden
to human beings, for example, Isaiah 55:10ff: 'As the heavens are
high above the earth, so are my ways above your ways'.[37]

If God remains radically inaccessible to human reason and
enquiry, if we ought not to 'scrutinise' God after the Arian
fashion, the question emerges logically, 'How can we know
anything about God?' The intellect has its own proper role for
Ephrem: it can enquire into those places where God has revealed
himself in creation.

> There is intellectual enquiry in the Church, investigating
> what is revealed: the intellect was not intended to pry into
> hidden things.[38]

Real knowledge of God unfolds in creation, grows in Holy
Scripture, and reaches its climax in the Incarnation. Divine love
for humankind is the motive that led God to bridge the
ontological chasm between Creator and creation in a process of
self-manifestation:

> Who, Lord, can gaze on your hiddenness
> which has come to revelation? Yes, your obscurity
> has come to manifestation and notification; your
> concealed Being
> has come out into the open, with limitation.
> Your awesome self has come into the hands
> of those who seized you.
> All this has happened to you, Lord,

because you became a human being.
Praises to him who sent you.
Yet you will not fear
because, even though your epiphany is revealed
and so too your human birth,
Your birth from the Father remains unattainable:
it has baffled all those who investigate it.[39]

Knowledge of God consists in a progressive revelation of God's *own self*. '...Ephrem considers revelation as a process engaging God himself in a sort of progressive incarnation. In imprinting in nature and Sacred Scripture the signs which reveal him, it is as if God were preparing to put on the human body of Jesus.'[40]

This connection for Ephrem of the revelation in creation and the revelation in Christ is integral: creation is revelatory because it was created by the Word himself:

> Where you look, the symbol of Christ is present. And where you read, you find his types. For it is by him that creatures have been made, and he has marked all his works by his symbols, since he created the world.[41]

If nothing can exhaust the mystery of God, then human language is necessarily inadequate in attempting to speak the mystery. Perhaps for this reason, and also because there is a tradition of feminine words for 'Spirit' in Semitic languages, feminine imagery is applied to the Trinity.[42] A particularly beautiful image has to do with the womb of the Father. Addressing Christ, Ephrem writes:

> If anyone seeks your hidden nature, behold it is in heaven in the great womb of Divinity. And if anyone seeks your revealed body, behold it rests and looks out from the small womb of Mary![43]

By 'divinity' in this passage Ephrem intends the Father. The Father in heaven has a 'great womb', which eternally generates the Son. The incarnation of the Son takes place in time in 'the small womb' of the Virgin Mary. A Western systematic thinker might be inclined to fault Ephrem here, in that from an analytic perspective it is clearly incongruous to talk about fathers having wombs, especially the Eternal Father. Poetry, however, does not operate in unambiguously lucid, analytic terms, but by way of allusion, heaping up images and metaphors, and through at least an implicit affirmation that logical analysis does not have the last word on human meaning. Brian McNeil summarises nicely this Syriac point of view:

> The fundamental theological perception here is that [this antithesis] when the discord is held and not prematurely resolved, reveals that God, who has clothed himself in human nature and so made it possible for us to speak of him, nevertheless remains beyond all human knowing and beyond all human discourse: his immanence in his creation, his presence in the history of Israel, and his incarnation in Jesus Christ, do not compromise his transcendence – nor does his transcendence compromise his immanence.'[44]

Ephrem and the Eucharist

Ephrem describes Christ as the 'medicine of life which flew down from on high'.[45] At the Last Supper,

> the lifegiver of all blessed the food,
> and it became the Medicine of Life
> for those who ate it.[46]

In similar fashion he writes about the eucharistic cup:

> The grape of mercy was pressed,
> and gave the Medicine of Life to the peoples.[47]

Ephrem seems to envisage daily communion when he writes:

> The assembly of the saints bears
> resemblance to Paradise:
> in it *each day*, is plucked the fruit
> of him who gives life to all.[48]

The paradisal motif is further developed by Ephrem in relation to the Eucharist:

> The spiritual bread of the Eucharist
> makes light and causes to fly:
> the peoples have been wafted up
> and have settled in paradise.
>
> Through the Second Adam who entered paradise
> everyone has entered it,
> for through the First Adam who left it
> everyone left it.
>
> By means of the spiritual bread
> everyone becomes an eagle who reaches
> as far as paradise.
> Whoever eats the living bread of the Son
> flies to meet him in the very clouds.[49]

Here the Pauline theme of the First Adam/Second Adam is allied to the Johannine theme of Christ as the living bread come down from heaven to give paradisal life to all who receive it. Ephrem's eucharistic theology is as saturated with Holy Scripture as is Cyprian's, but the concerns are somewhat different. Probably because martyrdom is largely a thing of the past when Ephrem is writing, the notion of sacrifice applied to the Eucharist is not so prominent in Ephrem. His biblical usage tends toward the

01326315

affirmation of a more intimate organic link between the Christian and Christ through reception of holy communion. Nor is there any lack of what we might call eucharistic realism in the mystical theology of Ephrem. This realism is finely brought out in a hymn in which he describes the eucharistic Christ as the 'Coal of Fire' in Isaiah's prophetic vision:

> The seraph could not touch the coal of fire with his fingers, and the coal merely touched Isaiah's mouth: the seraph did not hold it, Isaiah did not consume it, but our Lord has allowed us to do both.[50]

The eucharistic realism is developed even more when Ephrem describes how Christian life is to be lived in greater and ever greater conformity with Christ as we are assimilated to him in holy communion:

> Christ's body has newly been mingled with our bodies,
> His blood too has been poured out into our veins,
> His voice is in our ears,
> His brightness in our eyes.
> In his compassion the whole of him has been mingled
> in with the whole of us.[51]

Cyprian, Ephrem and today

An attempt has been made to outline the strict discipline of the North African bishop-theologian Cyprian and the poetic mysticism of the deacon-theologian Ephrem. How might we, listening across the centuries to the accents of theological truth in these two patristic theologians, relate to them so as to hear them speak to our ecclesial situation today? One way of doing this is to leap forward from the third and fourth centuries virtually to our own time and to enlist the theological and spiritual insights of the Austrian-English lay theologian, Baron Friedrich Von Hugel (1852-1925).

In a number of important books, especially *The Mystical Element of Religion, Eternal Life,* and *Essays and Addresses on the Philosophy of Religion,* Von Hugel developed the idea that religion is composed of three principal elements, which he termed the institutional, the mystical and the intellectual, and he maintained that interaction of all three was necessary for mature religion and faith.[52]

By the institutional element of religion, Von Hugel meant all the external structures, offices and officers by means of which a religion gets handed on from one generation to another. The institutional stands for the entire fabric of what is *observable* about a religion. He describes it thus:

> Behind every saint stands another saint. In vain do all the mystics, as such, vividly feel their experience to be utterly without human antecedent connection. Behind St Paul stands the Jewish synagogue and the earthly Jesus... Here is the abiding right and need of the Church, as the fellowship and training school of believers.[53]

The institutional element prevents religion from becoming too emotional or from freezing into a negative otherworldliness. It keeps religion earthed: 'Complete humility demands my continuous recognition of my own multiform need of my fellow-creatures, especially of those wiser and better than myself, and of my *lifelong need of training, discipline, incorporation... full humility requires filial obedience and docility towards men and institutions.*'[54] By the mystical element of religion, Von Hugel meant prayer, worship, personal relationship with God. With regard to the popular tendency to think of the mystical having to do with particularly extraordinary experiences, Von Hugel notes that the mystical exists '...in some form and degree in every mind'.[55] Being mystical is growing in continued awareness of God, and being transformed by that awareness and relationship. The mystical awareness, says Von Hugel, yields this perception:

'an absolute abidingness, pure simultaneity, eternity, in God…
stand out in man's deepest consciousness, with ever-painful
contrast, against all mere succession, all sheer flux and change'.[56]

By the intellectual element of religion Von Hugel intended
human reasoning, understanding, making sense of religion. It
consists of asking questions about all matters of one's faith, and
being prepared to seek answers to such questions that are coherent,
free of contradiction, and capable of being handed on to others.

Each of these three elements has its own particular
temptation, according to Von Hugel. The temptation of the
institutional is toward coercive power, and often causes
resentment and alienation; the temptation of the mystical is
superstition, a concentration on the subject that sits all too free
of objective reality; the temptation of the intellectual is
rationalism, setting oneself up as the sole arbiter of the real. At
the same time, the three elements have a common temptation
and that is to be considered as the *only* element.[57] On the level of
the individual's religion, the temptation consists in clinging to
one of the elements while evading the equally just and right
claims of the others. The proper relationship between the
institutional, the mystical and the intellectual elements of
religion is one of 'fruitful tension', and Von Hugel certainly
believed in what he called 'the spiritual benefits of friction'.

In terms of this essay both Cyprian and Ephrem instance, each
in his own way, each with his own particularity of expression, the
intellectual dimension of Christianity. Each seeks to present an
intelligible version of Christianity. For Cyprian the Holy
Scriptures and the Latin culture and theology of Tertullian inform
his perspective. For Ephrem the holy Scriptures and a non-
Western, Semitic culture and theology guide his exploration of
faith. It is also possible, however, to view Cyprian as exemplifying
the institutional dimension of Christianity far more obviously
than Ephrem. His emphasis on discipline, obedience, the unity of
the Church, authority, demonstrates the pastoral power of the

institution of the Church at work. Ephrem, on the other hand, reveals through his images and symbolism and especially through his poetic skill the mystical dimension of Christianity far more than Cyprian. At the same time, one can without difficulty find the institutional in Ephrem, and the mystical in Cyprian. It is a matter of degree, and of personal aptitude and orientation, as well as of social and cultural circumstances.

Knowing the great tradition of Cyprian and Ephrem, and so many others, prevents us losing our bearings in theology and theological education, prevents us falling prey to the heady but pseudo-charms of modernity. Appreciating the minds of Cyprian and Ephrem enables us to see what it means to keep faithful balance in the modern Church in its institutional, mystical and intellectual elements, without becoming clones one of another.

2

MEDIEVAL EUCHARISTIC THEOLOGY

Introduction

In the Catholic tradition one of the normative expressions of the 'real presence of Christ' occurs in the *Constitution on The Sacred Liturgy* of the Second Vatican Council, paragraph 7:

> To accomplish so great a work [of redemption] Christ is always present in his Church, especially in [its] liturgical celebrations. He is present in the sacrifice of the Mass not only in the person of his minister... but especially in the eucharistic species. By his power he is present in the sacraments so that when anybody baptises it is really Christ himself who baptises. He is present in his word since it is he himself who speaks when the holy Scriptures are read in the church. Lastly, he is present when the church prays and sings for he has promised 'where two or three are gathered together in my name, there am I in the midst of them'. (Mt 18:20)[1]

Clearly the Constitution is speaking of the many ways in which Christ is believed to be present. Even so, many Catholics continue to speak of the 'real presence' as coterminous with the eucharistic gifts, the consecrated bread and wine. Almost as though the Constitution needed further spelling out, Pope Paul VI added to this paragraph in *Mysterium fidei,* later taken up in the *Instruction on the Worship of the Eucharistic Mystery* (1967):

> For in this sacrament [of the Eucharist] Christ is present in a unique way, whole and entire, God and man, substantially and permanently. This presence of Christ under the species is called 'real', not in an exclusive sense, as if the other kinds of presence were not real, but *par excellence.*[2]

Why begin an essay on medieval eucharistic theology with these contemporary statements on the eucharistic presence of Christ? The answer is straightforward. The aim of this chapter is not to produce a fine exegesis of medieval eucharistic texts. Historians of doctrine are the people to do this, for example, Pelikan, Macy, Chadwick, Mitchell, whose works I have consulted and used. The aim is rather to explore something of what was going on in the medieval period, from the point of view of contemporary Catholic eucharistic theology and practice, and to see what lessons it may have for us today. The period to be examined is roughly from the ninth century to the thirteenth century, and the treatment will necessarily be selective, being guided by the pastoral nature of this essay.

Paschasius and Ratramnus

In the ninth century there were two monks of the Benedictine Abbey of Corbie, some ten miles to the east of Amiens, both of whom wrote books on the Eucharist. Their names were Paschasius Radbertus (c. 790-865) and his pupil Ratramnus (d. 868). Although both celebrated Eucharist together, received holy communion together, worshipped and prayed together, studied together, they produced two sharply contrasting eucharistic theologies in books bearing the same title, *De Corpore et Sanguine Domini*, 'On the Body and Blood of the Lord'.

Paschasius' book was written in 831 and has the distinction of being the first attempt that we know of in the Latin West to deal with the Eucharist in a systematic, doctrinal way. Patristic works which treat of the Eucharist tended to do so in its liturgical context, as the climax of Christian initiation, for example, in the 'Mystagogical Catechesis' of Cyril of Jerusalem or the writings of Theodore of Mopsuestia. Patristic authors did not probe very much into questions about change and presence in the Eucharist independently of its liturgical context.

Paschasius' contribution is his insistence on the utter realism of Christ's eucharistic presence. He could see almost no difference between the eucharistic body of Christ and the body of Jesus, born of the Virgin Mary:

> Just as the true flesh of Christ was created, without intercourse, from the Virgin through the Spirit, so through the same [Spirit], the same body and blood of Christ is mystically consecrated from the substance of bread and wine.

Hence he says indeed that this is nothing else than true flesh and true blood – although mystically (present).

This crude realism which Paschasius describes finds endorsement in his approval of various legends that speak of bleeding hosts.

> No one who reads the lives and deeds of the saints can remain unaware that often these mystical sacraments of the body and blood have been revealed under the visible form of a lamb of the actual colour of flesh and blood. This has been done either on behalf of the doubtful or on behalf of those who love Christ more fervently. In this way, Christ graciously offers faith to the unbelieving: When the gifts are broken or the host is offered, a lamb appears in the hands [of the priest] and blood flows in the chalice as at a sacrifice. What is thus hidden in mystery becomes manifest to doubters through a miracle.[3]

For all practical purposes, then, Paschasius sees the bread and wine almost as envelopes encasing the natural flesh and blood of Jesus. However, the communicant receiving and eating this real body of Christ does so 'mystically' and in a way that is not perceptible to the senses.

Paschasius' 'eucharistic materialism' is not, then,

thoroughgoing and total. He sensed the need for some theory of symbol or sacrament to avoid this kind of crude materialism, but he was unable to articulate it with a satisfactory degree of coherence. This was where his pupil in the monastery, Ratramnus, was somewhat more successful.

Ratramnus did not disagree with his teacher that Christ is present in the Eucharist, but he differed from him on how that presence was to be understood. Ratramnus eschewed any suggestion that the eucharistic body is the same as the historical body of Christ:

> We are taught that the body in which Christ suffered and the blood which flowed from his side as he hung on the cross differ greatly from this body which the faithful celebrate daily in the mystery of Christ's passion, and from this blood which the faithful drink, in order that it may be the mystery of that blood by which the world was redeemed.[4]

How does the historical body of Christ 'differ greatly' from the eucharistic body of Christ? Ratramnus provides what we might call an epistemology of the Eucharist. He distinguishes two ways of knowing. First, knowing *in veritate*, 'in truth', is knowledge through direct perception, knowledge of empirical reality. Secondly, knowing *in figura,* 'in figure-symbol', is knowledge through the symbolism of what is directly perceived.

Which category is appropriate for the eucharistic body and blood of Christ? Where Paschasius would have come close to the first category, Ratramnus is clear that it must be second, *in figura,* because the Eucharist is an action which 'exhibits one thing outwardly to the human senses and proclaims another thing inwardly to the minds of the faithful.'[5] Liam Walsh summarises the position of Ratramnus nicely:

According to this terminology the 'veritas' of the Eucharist is bread; the body of Christ is in the bread in 'figura', because it is perceived through the symbolism of the bread.[6]

Ultimately, the real issue between Paschasius and Ratramnus was philosophical: What is real? They both believed in the eucharistic presence of the Lord, but formulated that belief differently because of their varying philosophical positions about the nature of reality.

Berengar and Lanfranc

Essentially the same debate emerged again in the 11th century. The key figure was Berengar of Tours (c. 1010-1088). At a synod held in Rome in 1059 during the pontificate of Nicholas II, Berengar was forced to make the following confession of faith by Cardinal Humbert of Silva Candida:

> I, Berengarius... acknowledging the true apostolic faith, anathematise every heresy, especially that one for which heretofore I have been infamous: which [heresy] attempted to prove that the bread and wine which are placed on the altar remain merely a sacrament after consecration – not the true body and blood of our Lord Jesus Christ; and further, that [the body and blood] are touched and broken by the hands of the priest and crushed by the teeth of the faithful in a sacramental manner only – and not physically (*sensualiter*). I assent to the Holy Roman Church and the Apostolic See, and I confess with mouth and heart that... the bread and wine which are placed on the altar are not merely sacrament after consecration, but are rather the true body and blood of our Lord Jesus Christ – and that these are truly, physically and not merely sacramentally, touched and broken by the hands of the priests and crushed by the teeth of the faithful.[7]

The quite intense eucharistic realism of the confession, which became known in later canonical collections by its opening words 'Ego Berengarius', suggests that Berengar was understood to maintain that the eucharistic gifts of bread and wine were but mere symbols of the body and blood of Christ. I have expressed myself in this rather cumbersome way because it does not seem to me that Berengar was denying the eucharistic presence of Christ as such. He seems to have been working with a rough and ready empiricism which assumes that the reality of a thing is known by its appearances. If this is so, then a thing must be what it seems to be. If what on the altar looks like bread, tastes like bread, feels like bread, smells like bread – it must be bread. Yet Berengar believed that what was received in faith by the Christian was the body of Christ. Liam Walsh, again with admirable clarity, sums up Berengar's position:

> In his view what happens at the consecration is that, while continuing to be what it is, the bread begins to be the sign of the life-giving body of Christ that is thus present and eaten spiritually.[8]

The bread is the sign of Christ's life-giving body on christological grounds also. Christ's body has, through the glorification of the resurrection, gone beyond suffering and death, and so it cannot be injured by a priest's hands or a Christian's teeth.

Unfortunately, Berengar's opponents interpreted his sacramentalism as a denial of the reality or *veritas* of Christ's presence in the Eucharist. A crude realism, insisting that the bread was changed physically into the flesh of Christ, became the dominant Roman position which lies behind the statement Berengar had to sign at the Roman synod.

Is it possible also to see a certain growing 'ultramontanism' behind the confession? Sir Henry Chadwick writes that

the brilliant Cardinal Humbert figures among the earliest
exponents of the opinion that Roman primacy is the divinely
given organ through which an all too human church, prone to
limitless error and threatened by centrifugal force, is granted its
one effective guarantee of abiding in the right path.[9]

This is not in any way to deny the legitimacy and the
importance of the primacy of the pope as the focus of unity in
the universal church. Chadwick is rather pointing to the excessive
and exclusive centreing on the papacy by such a strong and
influential figure as Humbert with all its negative consequences.

In 1063, Lanfranc, abbot of the monastery of St Stephen in
Caen, wrote a reply to Berengar's eucharistic theology, *Liber de
Corpore et Sanguine Domini*, 'A Book Concerning the Body and
Blood of the Lord'. Lanfranc's understanding of eucharistic
theology was heavily influenced by the work of Ambrose of
Milan, especially by his sacramental realism.

On the presence of Christ, Lanfranc wrote:

> We believe that through the ministry of the priest, the
> earthly substances on the Lord's table are sanctified by
> divine power in a manner that is unspeakable,
> incomprehensible, marvellous; and that these substances
> are changed into the essence of the Lord's body, even
> though the appearance of earthly elements remains...[10]

If these earthly substances are changed into 'the essence of the
Lord's body,' how does Lanfranc cope with Berengar's
Christological objection that the glorified body of Christ is in
heaven? Quite simply, in typical Ambrosian style: if God can
create the universe out of nothing, then the Word can offer his
flesh to be broken and eaten on earth while it remains intact in
heaven. The power of God, and therefore of the Son, is the
central issue in this question, as Lanfranc sees it.

Transubstantiation and St Thomas Aquinas

As a result of the growing influence of Aristotelian thought, in the early third of the twelfth century the word *transubstantiation* came into vogue for describing the eucharistic change and presence. It seems that its first occurrence is in the *Book of Sentences* of Rolando Bandinelli, later to become Pope Alexander III, between 1140-41. But it was in the year 1215, at the Fourth Lateran Council, that the term first appeared in an official document of the Church:

> In this Church Jesus Christ is himself at once priest and sacrifice, whose body and blood are truly contained in the sacrament of the altar under the species of bread and wine, bread having been transubstantiated into his body, and wine into his blood.

Other modes of expression continued to be used to denote eucharistic presence, but transubstantiation began to predominate. It finds its finest expression in the *Summa Theologica* of Thomas Aquinas, IIIa, pp.75-77. There we read:

> The whole substance of the bread is changed into the whole substance of Christ's body, and the whole substance of the wine into the whole substance of Christ's blood. Hence, this conversion... may be designated by a name of its own, transubstantiation.

What we find in the Fourth Lateran Council, in Aquinas, and subsequently is an attempt to clarify language to avoid the crudities of the earlier eucharistic controversies and to affirm the eucharistic presence. Transubstantiation is a middle term, and a metaphysical one, expressing belief in the eucharistic presence, between Paschasian naive realism and supposed Berengarian symbolism.[11]

The Contribution of Gary Macy

One could be forgiven for thinking, on the basis of this essay, that the only significant feature of eucharistic theology in the medieval period was the eucharistic presence of Christ. It is the great merit of Gary Macy's book, *The Theologies of the Eucharist in the Early Scholastic Period*,[12] that it shows the variety of eucharistic theologies in the Middle Ages.

Macy suggests that it is useful to consider medieval eucharistic theology as expressive of three approaches: Paschasian, mystical, ecclesiastical. The first approach, the Paschasian, dealing with the issue of eucharistic presence, has formed the substance of this essay. It remains to say something about the other two.

In the mystical approach, the Eucharist is understood as a sign of the faith and love which unite God and the Christian. The real presence is never denied, but questions about the mode and manner of this presence are very much less pressing. It is the fruit of the Eucharist in the spiritual pilgrimage of the individual Christian that is the central focus of attention. The mystical approach is associated especially with the cathedral school of Laon and the school of St Victor in Paris.

To take but one example, Anselm of Laon (d. 1158) maintained that the consecrated elements are a sign of the spiritual union of the soul with God. The *res* of the sacrament, the reality behind the sign, is the spiritual union of the believer with God. This union, for Anselm, could be established even without actually receiving the consecrated elements. Needless to say, Anselm was not in any sense opposed to receiving holy communion. Rather, he exemplifies the growth of the devotional practice that has come to be called 'spiritual communion'.

The centre for the ecclesiastical approach was the school of Poitiers. Gilbert de la Porree (d. 1154) is perhaps its best known representative. For Gilbert, the reality of which the elements are an effective sign is not so much the personal, individual bond with Christ, as in the mystical approach, but the bond which unites all the saved, that is, the Church. Salvation is about spiritual union in faith and love but within the *communio* of the Church. The ecclesial unity is supremely and perfectly expressed in the celebration of the Eucharist, a theme close to the heart of the Second Vatican Council's *Constitution on the Sacred Liturgy.*

Macy does not suggest that these approaches to or models of eucharistic theology existed in some pure state in these schools or in individual theologians without overlap. They are best understood as theological tendencies or emphases, and their real value is to underscore the rich diversity of medieval eucharistic theology.

Conclusion

If unity in faith, but without uniformity of expression or emphasis, is the insight gained through Macy's meticulous research into medieval eucharistic theology, why have I concentrated for the most part on what he calls the Paschasian approach, the issue of eucharistic presence? My reason relates to the quotation from the *Constitution on the Sacred Liturgy* and from the *Instruction on the Worship of the Eucharistic Mystery* at the outset of this essay.

In essence what happened in the medieval period was that the focus shifted from the action of the Eucharist to the eucharistic elements on the altar-table. The whole manner of regarding the Eucharist shifted from the Jewish meal tradition, maintained and developed during the patristic period, to the sacred objects of the consecrated bread and wine. A cult of *looking* at the Eucharist effectively replaced the *doing* of the Eucharist by the entire Christian community, under the presidency of the ordained minister. It is in part to counteract this development that the Fourth Lateran Council required that the faithful receive Communion at least once a year.

Once this transition from doing to looking had taken place, it was virtually inevitable that the 'empirical' question (if that is the right term) of what precisely those elements are would be raised. In the Roman Catholic tradition we are still very much living with this Paschasian approach to the Eucharist, both in our theology at the popular level and in our eucharistic catechesis. If the affirmations of the Second Vatican Council and subsequent documents of the magisterium are to bear fruit in our pastoral ministry, then a very definite and determined effort is required to move on from this Paschasian to a more truly catholic and eucharistic practice and theology.

3

THE REFORMERS AND EUCHARISTIC ECCLESIOLOGY

Introduction

Eucharistic ecclesiology is a very fine conceptual key to assist in unlocking not only the riches of the Eucharist and the Church for Catholics, but also to aid the promotion of ecumenical dialogue. No one has demonstrated this more ably than Paul McPartlan. In *The Eucharist Makes the Church*[1] McPartlan offers us the fruit of his doctoral dissertation, comparing and contrasting the theologies of Henri de Lubac and John Zizioulas. In his *Sacrament of Salvation: An Introduction to Eucharistic Ecclesiology*[2] we are presented with a very rich synthesis of eucharistic ecclesiology, replete with ecumenical sensitivity and possibilities. With its axiom 'The Eucharist makes the Church and the Church makes the Eucharist', the Orthodox Churches are the natural and obvious dialogue partner for Catholicism when it comes to exploring and mining eucharistic ecclesiology.

While McPartlan does attend to the Lima Statement in chapter six of *Sacrament of Salvation*, the reformers and the Reformation tradition are not particularly obvious in his presentation of eucharistic ecclesiology. To some extent this is understandable in that the Eucharist and the Church are both issues fraught with tension and polemics in the sixteenth century. The issue becomes even more complex when one considers not only the vast amount of writing – books, pamphlets, catechisms, sermons, letters – generated by the principal reformers themselves, but also their intention to define their theologies against both the Catholic Church and one another. It is the contention of this chapter, however, that despite the acknowledged complexity of the task and the risks inherent in reading the reformers selectively and through one's own eucharistic-ecclesial lenses, it is possible to demonstrate elements of a eucharistic ecclesiology in Luther, Zwingli and Calvin. 'Elements' is the key word here. No attempt is made to articulate a fully developed theology of either the Church or the Eucharist in the reformers. Rather, the objective is to show close connections between Eucharist and Church in some of their writings.

Martin Luther (1483-1546)[3]

In his 1520 treatise, *On the Papacy in Rome,* his first writing to deal explicitly with the Church, Luther contrasts the real meaning of Church as the gathering of those who, in the Spirit, believe in Christ, with external forms of Christendom. The former is to the latter as soul is to body.[4] He is not thereby opposed to the 'external' nature of the Church, but principally to the abuse of power and authority and, in fact, in the 1520s, when the *Schwaermer* or enthusiasts showed themselves opposed to ecclesiastical structures generally, Luther wrote against them.[5] Because 'the one, eternal and unmistakable mark of the Church is, and always has been the Word',[6] the Church is essentially itself as the community gathered around the Word of God.[7] The Church, for Luther, is also the communion of saints 'with the appearance of a sinner',[8] and eucharistic communion is the sign of personal incorporation with Christ and his saints in both blessings and sufferings:

> This fellowship consists in this, that all the spiritual possessions of Christ and his saints are shared with and become the property of him who receives this sacrament. Again, all sufferings and sins also become common property; and thus love engenders love in return and mutual love unites.[9]

The Eucharist becomes the sacrament that enables the bearing of one another's burdens within the whole mystical body of Christ. There is a purple passage in Luther, expressing this idea very finely, that deserves to be quoted at length:

> Whoever is in despair, distressed by a sin-stricken conscience or terrified by death or carrying some other burden upon his heart, if he would be rid of them all, let him go joyfully to the sacrament of the altar and lay down his woe in the midst of the community [of saints] and seek help from the entire company of the spiritual body – just as a citizen who has suffered damage or misfortune at the hands of his enemies makes complaint to the town council and fellow citizens and asks them for help. The immeasurable grace and mercy of God are given us in this sacrament to the end that we might put from us all misery and tribulation and lay it upon the community [of saints], and especially upon Christ... Here your heart must go out in love and learn that this is a sacrament of love. As love and support are given to you, you in turn must render love and support to Christ in his needy ones. You must feel with sorrow all the dishonour done to Christ in his holy Word, all the misery of Christendom, all the unjust suffering of the innocent, with which the world is everywhere filled to overflowing. You must fight, work, pray and – if you cannot do more – have heartfelt sympathy. See, this is what it means to bear in your turn the misfortune and adversity of Christ and his saints. It is as if he were saying 'I am the Head, I will be the first to give himself for you... And I leave you this sacrament, as a sure token of all this, in order that you may not forget me, but daily call to mind and admonish one another by means of what I did, and I am still doing for you, in order that you may be strengthened, and also bear one another in the same way.'[10]

Behind this thinking, and indeed so much else in Luther, lies a profound mystical sense of union with Christ. The Lutheran specialist Heiko Oberman comments:

> ...it is highly precarious to separate the mystical tissue from the living organism of Luther's spirituality. The tissue of mysticism cannot be treated as one aspect of Luther's theology... but is part and parcel of his overall understanding of the gospel itself and therefore pervades his understanding of faith, justification, hermeneutics, *ecclesiology* and pneumatology.'[11]

This 'in-Christ' mysticism is fundamentally ecclesial for Luther. Thus, Christ lives and is at work in believers:

> For as Christ is crucified, so he also rises, sleeps, wakes, acts, and rests in us.[12]

Contrasting his own position with that of the *Schwaermer* who see the risen Christ only at God's right hand in heaven, Luther writes:

> Therefore, in him we live and move and have our being (Ac 17:28). Hence the speculation of the sectarians is vain when they imagine that Christ is present in us 'spiritually', that is speculatively, but is present really in heaven. Christ and faith must be completely joined. We must simply take our place in heaven; and Christ must be, live and work in us. But he lives and works in us, not speculatively but really, with presence and power.[13]

A firm believer in the real presence of Christ in the eucharistic elements, Luther insists that this mystical union comes about through eating and drinking the consecrated bread and wine of the Lord's Supper:

For there is no more intimate, deep and indivisible union of the food [Christ] with him who is fed [the communicant]. For the food enters into and is assimilated by his very nature, and becomes one substance with the person who is fed.[14]

This ecclesial approach to the Eucharist, so dominant in the early Luther especially, gives way in his later writings, under pressure of controversy with Carlstadt, Zwingli and others, to the real presence of Christ, though it is never entirely absent.[15] For Luther, Christ is in the Christian, with all the other saints in the mystical body, through the Eucharist.

Huldrych Zwingli (1484-1531)

Probably one of the best known aspects of Zwingli's theology has to do with his minimalist position on the real presence of Christ in the Eucharist during his Marburg Colloquy in 1529 with Martin Luther and various other reformers. Luther was defending the real presence of Christ in the eucharistic gifts against a reductionist Zwingli who denied it, a defence which was later to earn for Luther the nickname 'Dr Pussyfoot' among those Protestants who judged his break with Catholicism to be less than complete.[16]

The eminent Zwingli scholar, W. Peter Stephens, maintains that most of Zwingli's eucharistic theology was in place, at least implicitly, in 1524, five years before the Marburg Colloquy.[17] If we turn to Zwingli's 1524 *Letter to Matthew Alber*, the Reutlingen reformer, whose eucharistic theology is by and large regarded as representative of Luther's, we find the broad lineaments of Zwingli's thinking.[18] The first part of the letter focuses on John 6, and in his comments Zwingli attempts to show that 'eating Christ' does not and cannot mean literally what it says. Rather, it means 'believing in Christ'. The key text for Zwingli is John 6:63:

It is the spirit that gives life, the flesh is of no avail; the words that I have spoken to you are spirit and life.

He is attempting to defend and safeguard the central Reformation principle that salvation is by grace and faith alone, and so God-in-Christ comes first, and not the sacramental rites of the Church. 'From an exegetical point of view, he believes that the spiritualistic interpretation of the Supper as feeding on Christ by faith is the authentic biblical understanding, which later became overloaded with a sacramental interpretation from which it ought now to be detached.'[19] In the second part of the letter he comments on the words of consecration, 'This is (*est*) my body'. Following a suggestion of the Dutch humanist, Cornelisz Hoen, who had written to both him and Luther, Zwingli suggests that *est* means *significat*, that is, 'signifies'. 'Put 'signifies' for 'is' here and you have 'Take, eat; this signifies my body which is given for you.' Then the meaning will certainly be 'Take, eat, for this which I bid you do will signify to you or remind you of my body which presently is to be given for you.'[20] The bread represents or signifies Christ's body, so that when it is eaten, it calls to remembrance that Christ gave his body, gave himself, for us. This interpretation certainly contrasts with the more traditional interpretation of real presence found in Luther and about which they could not reach agreement in the Marburg Colloquy.

However, there is more to Zwingli's eucharistic theology than that. If his exegesis of John 6 led him to a symbolical understanding of the real presence of Christ in the eucharistic gifts, and consequently to a spiritualistic appreciation of eating and drinking those gifts, his exegesis of 1 Corinthians 10:16-17 brought him to a much deeper appreciation of the ecclesial dimension of the Eucharist:

...they who here eat and drink are one body, one bread; that is, all those who come together to proclaim Christ's death and eat the symbolic bread, declare themselves to be Christ's body, that is, members of his Church; and as this Church holds one faith and eats one symbolical bread, so it is one bread and one body.[21]

Further, Jacques Courvoisier, in a most lucid presentation of Zwingli's theology, building upon the more recent work of less accessible Reformation specialists, drew attention to a proposal made by Zwingli in 1525 for the liturgy of Holy Communion, a liturgy for which the Zurich civil authorities refused permission.[22] The eucharistic prayer was replaced with an exchange between the pastor and his assistants, and an antiphonal exchange between the men and women of the congregation, seated on separate sides of the nave. A simple wooden table was placed in the nave, in contrast to the altar in the chancel, and the eucharistic vessels were also wooden. The communicants were to receive communion from the servers with their own hands. Prior to the reception of communion, this prayer is offered:

> O Lord God Almighty, who by thy Spirit hast brought us together into thy *one body*, in the unity of faith, and hast commanded that *body* to give thee praise and thanks for thy goodness and free gift in delivering thine only begotten Son, our Lord Jesus Christ, to death for our sins: grant that we may do the same so faithfully that we may not, by any pretense or deceit, provoke thee who art the truth which cannot be deceived. Grant also that we may live as purely as *becometh thy body*, thy family and thy children, so that even the unbelieving may learn to recognise thy name and glory. Keep us, Lord, that thy name and glory may never be reviled because of our lives, O Lord, ever increase our faith, which is trust in thee, thou who livest and reignest, God for ever and ever. Amen.[23]

This liturgy, according to Courvoisier, expresses the conviction that the entire eucharistic assembly is transubstantiated into the body of Christ. 'Transubstantiation no longer concerns the bread, but the whole congregation, and it is *this* "body of Christ" which the congregation offers in oblation to its Lord.'[24] It is this transubstantiated community which is the real presence in Zwingli's eucharistic community.[25] For Zwingli, the Christian is fed and sustained as the body of Christ in and through the Eucharist.

John Calvin (1509-1564)

The entire *œuvre* of John Calvin may be described as a eucharistic theology, shot through with the themes of grace and gratitude.[26] All good things come to us from their graceful source in God, according to Calvin:

> It is not enough simply to hold that God is one who should be worshipped and adored by all, unless we are persuaded also that he is the fountain of all good, so that we should seek nothing anywhere else but in him. I take this to mean not only that he sustains this world, as he once established it, by his boundless power, governs it by his wisdom, preserves it by his goodness, and in particular rules the human race by his justice and judgment, supports it in his mercy, looks after it with his protection; but also that not one drop of wisdom and light, or justice, or power or uprightness, or genuine truth will be found that does not flow from him, and of which he is not the cause.... And so we should learn to look for, and to ask for, all these things from him, and when we receive them to ascribe them thankfully to him.[27]

God's abundant grace, his very being imparting himself in love is what we as creatures find all around us, and the only appropriate response is eucharistic, that is, one of sheer gratitude. Man, for Calvin, is essentially 'eucharistic man'.[28] The world of nature is unable to express its gratitude towards God for existence, to be eucharistic, but human beings can.

> In Calvin's view, it is this that make humans the apex of creation: the whole created order has it meaning and purpose in the praise that they alone, of all God's earthly creatures, can return to him, and his design in making the entire order of nature would be subverted if at any time there were no people to call upon him.[29]

The climax of God's gracious self-donation to us is the person of Jesus Christ. He is God's ultimate good gift. 'This is the purpose of the gospel,' maintains Calvin, 'that Christ should become ours, and that we should be ingrafted into his body.'[30] This ingrafting enables a mystical union with Christ, which is fundamental to his theology:

> We become truly members of his body, and life flows into us from him as from the head. For in no other way does he reconcile us to God by the sacrifice of his death than because he is ours and we are one with him.... How this happens, I confess is something far above the measure of my intelligence. Hence, I adore this mystery rather than labour to understand it.... He dwells in us, sustains us, gives us life and fulfils all the functions of the head.[31]

As Brian Gerrish rightly notes, in all of this use is being made of eucharistic language prior to any treatment of the Eucharist as such.[32]

The instrument or vehicle by which the gift that is Jesus Christ is given to us is the Word or the gospel, which is in turn the instrument of the Holy Spirit.[33] Pneumatology, christology and sacramental theology are closely inter-linked in Calvin's theology. If the Word or the gospel is the instrument of the Spirit in bringing the gift of Christ to us, what is the function of the sacraments? For Calvin, following St Augustine's description of a sacrament as a 'visible word', the sacraments represent visibly or graphically the Word preached.[34] Gerrish summarises Calvin's perspective nicely:

> ...if the sacraments confer no more than the Word, it is equally clear to Calvin that they confer no less. The sacraments have the same function as the Word of God: to offer and to present to us Jesus Christ. In other words, the sacraments, like preaching, are the vehicle of Christ's self-communication, of the real presence.[35]

'Calvin's doctrine of the Lord's Supper is a complex mixture of several motifs.'[36] These words of Gerrish signal for the systematic theologian something of the task involved in making an analysis of Calvin's eucharistic theology. It is the intention of this chapter, as stated above, simply to draw attention to some elements of his teaching that reflect a eucharistic ecclesiology. The Lord's Supper sustains and deepens the communion with Christ that has been established through the Word and baptism:

> For as God, regenerating us in baptism, ingrafts us into the fellowship of the Church, and makes us his by adoption, so... he performs the office of a provident parent in continually supplying the food by which he may sustain and preserve us in the life to which he has begotten us by his Word.[37]

This eucharistic sustenance is eschatologically oriented. It is 'a help by which we may be ingrafted into the body of Christ, or, already ingrafted, may be more and more united to him, until the union is completed in heaven.'[38] In summary, then, God gifts us with Jesus Christ, his perfect self-expression, through Word and sacrament by the power of the Holy Spirit, and sustains us in communion with this same Jesus until through grace that communion is perfected in heaven.

Conclusion

Four agreed statements have been produced in the Catholic-Orthodox dialogue so far: *The Mystery of the Church and of the Eucharist in the Light of the Mystery of the Holy Trinity* (1982); *Faith, Sacraments and the Unity of the Church* (1987); *The Sacrament of Order in the Sacramental Structure of the Church* (1988); *Uniatism, Method of Union of the Past, and the Present Search for Full Communion* (1993).[39] Much ecumenical hope is engendered by these statements, rooted as they are in the historic traditions of Orthodoxy and Catholicism. Perhaps, in a similar fashion, more hope for healing with and within the Churches of the Reformation would be possible by a return to the sources of Reformation theology in a common search for elements of a eucharistic ecclesiology.[40]

4

POPE PIUS X TO THE SECOND VATICAN COUNCIL

Introduction

Twentieth-century Catholicism before the Second Vatican Council was less monochrome, more complex, more richly theological than some would have us believe. Indeed, an adequate exegesis of the conciliar texts, especially with regard to their sources, would establish them as well anchored in the statements and documents of the magisterium and of theologians in this century.

Gabriel Daly, the Irish systematic and historical theologian, in a series of articles in *The Tablet* in 1981, likens the Catholic Church between the First (1870) and the Second Vatican Councils (1962-65) to a village with a high wall surrounded on the outside by jungle. This ecclesial village has been specially designed to preserve the last remnants of classical and medieval culture from the 'jungle' of bewildering modern ideas that had grown up and proliferated since the Enlightenment. However the world outside the village would be beset by the uncontrollable jungle growth of new ideas and thinking, the ecclesial village would be preserved intact and kept free from these destructive ways. The Second Vatican Council breached the wall surrounding the village of Catholicism at several points, and new ideas and thinking began to make their way into the village to alter its life.

One has to admit that there is a degree of truth in Daly's analogy, but, at least with respect to the Eucharist, it presents too uniform and too lifeless a view of pre-conciliar Catholicism. To show something of this range and richness of pre-conciliar eucharistic thought, this chapter will explore the contributions of Popes Pius X and Pius XII and of the theologians Anscar Vonier and Romano Guardini.

Pope Pius X (1903-14)

Two documents, in particular, emanating from the pontificate of Pope Pius X have to do with the Eucharist: *Sacra Tridentina Synodus* (1905) and *Quam Singulari* (1910). These, however, do not exhaust his interest in this liturgy. Pius' *motu proprio* on church music, *Tra le Sollecitudini* of 1903, for the first time used the words 'active participation of the faithful', later to become a leitmotif for the *Constitution on the Sacred Liturgy*. Thomas Bokenkotter notes that these words provided inspiration for the Belgian Benedictine, Dom Lambert Beauduin, to set out his challenge at the Catholic Congress of Malines in 1909:

> The people must share in the liturgy…[1]

It is this fundamental sharing of the people in the liturgy that lay behind Pius' two eucharistic decrees. The decree *Sacra Tridentina Synodus* (On The Daily Reception of Holy Communion), issued on 22 December 1905, took its opening words from the Council of Trent:

> The holy council wishes indeed that at each Mass the faithful who are present should communicate, not only in spiritual desire, but sacramentally, by the actual reception of the Eucharist.[2]

This strong commendation of holy communion is a constant throughout the tradition. Not only Trent, but the Fourth Lateran Council in 1215 stand as its conciliar witness. However, residual Jansenism still plagued the nineteenth- and twentieth-century Church, despite its condemnation in 1653. Jansenist anthropology, undoubtedly influenced to some degree by Calvinism, viewed human nature as radically corrupt and completely vitiated. Moral rigorism was one of the major consequences of this theological pessimism, and in respect of the

Eucharist, naturally, frequent reception was judged to be most inappropriate. It is this residual Jansenism that forms the backdrop to the papal decree.

Of the recommendations in the decree, some of them are especially noteworthy and speak as much to post-Second Vatican Council Catholics as to their forebears in 1905. Frequent and daily communion should be open to all the faithful, provided they have 'a right and devout intention', and a right and devout intention consists in the 'wish to please God, to be more closely united with him by charity and to have recourse to this divine remedy for... weakness and defects'.[3]

The language of 'right and devout intention' is important in order to underscore the meaning of our holy communion, especially in our time when frequent reception of holy communion is well established in the Church. It can never be permitted to degenerate into a convention, something that is simply expected when Mass is celebrated, with the appropriate disposition and preparation on the part of the individual. If rigorism is the defect of Jansenism, perhaps a certain casualness is our contemporary eucharistic defect.

The decree explicitly speaks of appropriate preparation and thanksgiving for holy communion. One notices also the emphasis that communion is a 'divine remedy for... weakness and defects'. The Eucharist not only celebrates our ecclesial identity as the body of Christ, but provides the support and strength necessary to live out the implications of that identity.

The decree *Quam Singulari* (On The Age for Admission to First Communion), issued on 10 August 1910, while acknowledging that the communion of young children, 'even sucklings', was well established historically in the tradition, notes that it had had become obsolete in the Latin Church. The Fourth Lateran Council prescribed reception of the sacraments of Penance and Eucharist for all the faithful 'after coming to the use of reason' at last once a year. In the following centuries, one age tended to be established for Penance and another for Eucharist, a practice frowned upon by the pope.

The central issue that engages the pope in the decree is lowering the age for receiving holy communion, and here again he finds residual Jansenism the culprit:

> Such injury is caused by those who insist on an extraordinary preparation for first holy communion, more than is reasonable, not realising, who maintain that holy Eucharist is a reward, not a remedy for human frailty.[4]

Again, as in *Sacra Tridentina Synodus,* is found the notion of Eucharist as remedy. The Eucharist as remedy, *pharmakon* in Greek, is found most especially in Ignatius of Antioch, but also in later patristic authors such as Clement of Alexandria, Serapion of Thmuis, and Gregory of Nazianzus.[5] Though the sources may not be explicitly identified in the decree, there is a clear retrieval of eucharistic tradition here.

When a child attains the use of reason, that is, when the eucharistic bread may be distinguished from common bread, then the child may be admitted to holy communion. The decree also comments on the knowledge of the faith required for first communion:

> A perfect knowledge of the articles of faith is therefore, not necessary...[6]

Recognising the step forward taken by Pope Pius X, some now feel that a similar step needs to be taken for the sacrament of Confirmation.[7]

Pope Pius XII (1939-58)
Three documents concerning the Eucharist from the pontificate of Pope Pius XII demand attention: *Mystici Corporis* (1943),

Mediator Dei (1947) and *Christus Dominus* (1953). The encyclical *Mystici Corporis* (The Mystical Body of Christ) is important for an understanding of Catholic ecclesiology in the twentieth century, and repays careful reading in its own right, but in the context of this chapter I shall focus only on a few paragraphs. Paragraph 19 is particularly fine:

> ...for in the holy Eucharist the faithful are nourished and grow strong at the same table, and in a divine ineffable way are brought into union with each other and with the divine head of the whole body. Finally, like a devoted mother the Church is at the beside of those who are sick unto death; and if it be not always God's will that by the sacred anointing of the sick [it] restore health to this mortal body, yet [it] does minister supernatural medicine for wounded souls, and sends new citizens on to heaven to enjoy forever the happiness of God – new advocates assigned to [it][8]

The final part of the paragraph affirms the union of Christ, the divine head, with his body, the Church. The motif has been a constant in the tradition since it first found expression in 1 Corinthians 12, and in many ways it is the essence of the encyclical. But in the second part of the paragraph is found the idea of the Eucharist as remedy/supernatural medicine/*pharmakon,* similar in expression to Pope Pius X. Both documents of Pius X were published within the decade prior to the First World War, which witnessed an enormous arms build-up in Europe and demonic power struggles. *Mystici Corporis* saw the light of day during the course of the Second World War, with all its self-evident horrors. It is tempting to see this emphasis of both popes on the Eucharist as a remedy/*pharmakon* speaking with a particular power to the manifest sickness of human beings that both caused and found expression in these horrendous global conflicts. Pope Pius XII also comes close to saying something like this in paragraph 83 of *Mystici Corporis:*

If in the sad and anxious days through which we are passing there are many who cling so firmly to Christ the Lord hidden beneath the eucharistic veils that neither tribulation nor distress nor famine nor nakedness nor danger nor persecution nor the sword can separate them from his love, then undoubtedly holy communion, which once again in God's providence is much more frequented even from days of early childhood, may become a source of courage that makes heroes out of Christians.[9]

Pope Pius XII's *Mediator Dei* (The Sacred Liturgy) is rightly regarded as a milestone in the renewal of the liturgy during this century, and as a forerunner of *Sacrosanctum Concilium*. There are many obvious links and continuities of thought between *Mystici Corporis* and *Mediator Dei*. Nowhere more than in the Eucharist, insists Pius XII, is the union of the head with the members of his mystical body clearly signified and nurtured (§31), so that Eucharist is 'the culmination and centre, as it were, to the Christian religion'.[10] At the same time, the pope is emphatic that the foundational value of the Eucharist cannot really be appropriated by the faithful without regular prayer and devotion (§32) and preparation for and thanksgiving after Mass (§126).

The various forms of devotion to the Eucharist – holy hours, the forty hours devotion, benediction – are strongly encouraged (§131-135). Though the pope does not use the actual term, he seems to have a vision of 'eucharistification' of the world, a vision deeply rooted in the mystical tradition and exemplified in the writings of his (at that time) unsung contemporary, Pierre Teilhard de Chardin. For Teilhard, with the consecrated host always as his starting-point and always as the controlling factor in his eucharistic vision, it is possible to contemplate the Divine Presence flowing throughout the universe, as it were.

The Host is like a burning hearth from which flames

spread and radiate. As the spark thrown into the briars is soon surrounded by a circle of fire, so, throughout the centuries, the sacramental Host (for there is but one Host growing ever greater in the hands of priests as one follows after another), the Host of bread, I repeat, is continually more closely surrounded by another Host, infinitely greater, which is nothing less than the universe itself, the universe gradually absorbed by the universal Element.[11]

This is no nature mysticism, as some critics of Teilhard alleged, but a vision of the eucharistification of the entire world, being gracefully drawn to the Parousia.

Finally, in *Christus Dominus* (On The New Discipline for the Eucharistic Fast), Pius XII altered the regulations governing the eucharistic fast. A theological and an experiential argument are brought forward by the pope to justify the practice of fasting before receiving holy communion. The theological argument turns to the tradition and recognises the widespread reality of eucharistic fasting from the fourth century onwards. The experiential argument tells us that 'when the body is not burdened with food the mind is rendered more alert and is more strongly moved to meditate on that sublime and hidden mystery...'.[12] At the same time, the pope acknowledges the difficulties experienced by people in maintaining the absolute fast, modifies it to some degree, and permits the celebration of Mass during the afternoon. In this way Pius XII resonates with the intentions of Pius X, to render the Eucharist accessible to people.

This is a major eucharistic concern of the magisterium in the twentieth century. The Eucharist cannot be accessible to the members of Christ's mystical body if they are preoccupied with a debilitating sense of unworthiness, or if they cannot receive until a later age, or if the discipline of fasting in a changing socio-economic world makes it particularly difficult. If the Eucharist is genuinely to be a remedy for people, if the Eucharist is to *make* the Church, in Henri de Lubac's admirable phrase, the people of the Church must obviously be able to receive it. This is the real eucharistic achievement of Popes Pius X and Pius XII.

Dom Anscar Vonier (1875-1938)

The Benedictine theologian and abbot of Buckfast Abbey, Dom Anscar Vonier, was ordained a priest in 1898, five years before the pontificate of Pope Pius X. He died in 1938, one year before the pontificate of Pope Pius XII. He is a good example of English-speaking eucharistic theology during the period we are considering.

Vonier wrote a number of works on dogmatic theology in a style which rendered abstruse questions in theology intelligible to the informed lay reader. His 1925 book, *A Key to the Doctrine of the Eucharist,* represents Vonier at his best, and it has been described by Aidan Nichols as 'a classic example of the best twentieth-century eucharistic theology'.[13] The key that Vonier offers to the doctrine of the Eucharist is the concept of sacramentality, taken essentially from Thomas Aquinas. Long before Edward Schillebeeckx popularised the notion in his *Christ the Sacrament,* Vonier had this to say:

> Sacraments are, through their very nature, an extension of the incarnation, a variant of that mystery expressed in the words: 'and the Word was made flesh and dwelt amongst us.' Is not the Son of God made man the sacrament *par excellence,* the *magnum sacramentum,* the invisible made visible?[14]

Writing at a time when there was considerable controversy about the relation of the Mass to Calvary, Vonier stays with Aquinas' notion of sacrament in order to explicate the relation. He distances himself from the extreme realists, perhaps ultra-realists, who end 'by explaining the Mass in terms of person, no longer in terms of sacrament'.[15] Vonier has appropriated too finely the mind of Thomas to fall into any version of ultra-realism, and so he concludes:

> St Thomas is too keen and too clear-headed a sacramentalist ever to become an ultra-realist; even when he says that Christ is immolated in the sacrament, his whole mode of thinking is sacramental... not natural.... When one sees how constant has been the tendency of pious men to slip from sacramental thought into natural thought one cannot help admiring St Thomas, who does not show one single instance of such a lapse.[16]

In an age which, because of rapid change and consequent insecurity, is all too prone to seek God in special events and physical-natural signs, Vonier stands as a prophetic warning. Eucharistic change has to do with the order of sacramentality, not with the order of physics and chemistry.

When he comes to describe the eucharistic presence of Christ, Vonier once again finds the key to the doctrine in the concept of sacramentality. Following Aquinas, he insists that Christ is not located 'on so many altars, as in so many places, but as in the sacrament.... The thing, the body of Christ, is not taken hold of, hurried through space and put into a definite place on a definite altar; this is not Eucharist at all; but the divine invocation... makes the substance of a definite cup of wine into a new thing, and what is that new thing? It is simply that thing which is in heaven, the body and blood of Christ, but which, not for one instant, has left heaven.'[17] Vonier held firmly to the definite understanding of transubstantiation, but the solidity of this grasp of sacramentality suggests that he would have been open to other philosophical attempts to express ontologically the belief in eucharistic change and presence. Vonier had no time for eucharistic ultra-realism, which he would have seen as characteristically Protestant. Sacramentalism is a *via media* for him, as indeed it was for Thomas in the backdrop of early medieval eucharistic controversies discussed above in chapter 2.

Romano Guardini (1885-1968)

Guardini forms a good contrast to Vonier. While the latter was radically indebted to Aquinas, Guardini was not. Mark Schoof writes:

> In the heyday of neo-scholasticism, it was almost impossible not to choose medieval thinkers as the subject of one's thesis, but Guardini twice refused to consider Thomas Aquinas and instead chose his opponent Bonaventure who was the medieval representation of the stricter Augustinian tradition.[18]

Guardini wrote a magisterial volume of only ninety pages with the title *The Spirit of the Liturgy,* and while it deals with the liturgy in general, everything he says may be applied specifically to the Eucharist.

In his book Guardini considers both the playfulness of the liturgy and the seriousness of the liturgy. He describes the mindset of many modern people characterised by a sense of purpose and by utilitarianism:

> Grave and earnest people, who make the knowledge of truth their whole aim, see moral problems in everything, and seek for a definite purpose everywhere, tend to experience a peculiar difficulty where the liturgy is concerned. They incline to regard it as being to a certain extent aimless, as a superfluous pageantry of a needlessly complicated and artificial character. They are affronted by the scrupulously exact instructions which the liturgy gives on correct procedure, on the right direction in which to turn, on the pitch of the voice, and so on. What is the use of it all?[19]

The liturgy for Guardini is in a special sense free from purpose and is, in the strict sense of the word, 'use-less'. 'It's not a means which is adapted to a certain end – it is an end in itself.'[20] In the liturgy the person is not intended to edify himself so much as to contemplate God's majesty. The best analogies for the liturgy are the play of a child and the creation of the artist. Play is 'life, pouring itself forth without an aim, and art is giving life to the being and longings of the artist, giving external shape to his inner truth. Through the liturgy and under the guidance of the Church, human beings "grow into living works of art before God"…'.[21]

In no way, however, is Guardini reducing the liturgy to aestheticism. 'Truth is the soul of beauty.'[22] Beauty isolated from moral goodness and from truth is for Guardini a misconstrual of beauty. The beautiful play of the liturgy, if indeed it is to be beautiful, must be harnessed to a life marked by the pursuit of truth and doing goodness. This is what Guardini means by the seriousness of the liturgy, and ultimately he anchors it in the words of the Lord: 'Seek first the kingdom of God and justice, and all shall be added to you – all else, even the glorious experience of beauty.'[23]

According to Karl Rahner, Guardini's successor in the Chair of Christianity and the Philosophy of Religion at Munich, Guardini confessed that he had been traumatised during the period of modernism and anti-modernism under Pope Pius X, and that 'he never got completely over it'.[24] There is no reason to doubt Rahner's reminiscence, but Guardini seems to have overcome his trauma to no small degree. He must be counted one of the most distinguished Catholic theologians of this century. In his autobiographical notes he tells how, as a student, he found his faith slipping away from him and how he found it again step by step. As he refound his faith, he also found the need for the truth of Jesus Christ to be objective. The objective form of that truth was for Guardini the Catholic Church. Whatever he may have suffered during the modernist-antimodernist period, Guardini never abandoned the Church. The love for his Church, not uncritical, was the key to his life as a priest and a theologian.[25] This love for the Church climaxes in *The Spirit of the Liturgy*, the spirit of playful contemplation of the beauty of God.

Conclusion

Even this cursory investigation of the eucharistic thought of two popes and two theologians in the twentieth century prior to the Second Vatican Council establishes something of the diversity of that period. Four very different priest-theologians with contrasting insights: Popes Pius X and Pius XII, anxious to make the Eucharist accessible to the faithful, and taking appropriate measures to do so; Anscar Vonier, retrieving the eucharistic sanity of Thomas Aquinas at a time of polemics and ultra-realism; Romano Guardini speculating about the playfulness of the liturgy. Each of them in his own fashion helped to pave the way for the liturgical renewal of the Council. Each of them recognised the centrality of the Eucharist for the tradition that is Catholicism. The achievement of all of them is best seen as the retrieval of the best of eucharistic doctrine in the previous nineteen centuries.[26]

5

THE SECOND VATICAN COUNCIL (1962-65)

Introduction

There can be no real dispute that the single most important event in twentieth-century Catholicism was the Second Vatican Council, 1962-65. Disputes, however, are readily available with regard to the interpretation and reception of the Council. Many of these disputes are, at least in part, based on a selective reading and a superficial interpretation of the Council documents. A careful reading of the footnotes to the documents and more than a nodding acquaintance with the history of Catholic theology would lead inescapably to the conclusion that the documents are rooted in tradition. Indeed, Robert Imbelli goes so far as to say:

> Were I asked to state briefly the major theological achievement of the Second Vatican Council, I would unhesitatingly reply: the recovery of *tradition.* There are two inseparable aspects of this. On the one hand, there was the rediscovery, thanks to careful historical labours of the 1940s and '50s, of rich veins of liturgical and ecclesial tradition antedating the 'traditional Catholicism' of the post-Reformation Church. On the other hand, there was the even more radical realisation that tradition is as much process as content (*tradition* as well as *tradita*), and that this process is living, creative and community-based.[1]

Imbelli's point is well-taken because too often the attempt is made to draw a superficial distinction between the pre-conciliar and post-conciliar Church as though the latter were a *new* Church that had rediscovered the Gospel that had been abandoned by the old Church.

Walter Kasper helpfully describes three phases of development after the council: the phase of exuberance, as a variety of changes, especially in the liturgy, became implemented; a phase of disappointment, as liberals failed to experience the fulfilment of their expectations, and conservatives talked about signs of dissolution; and a new phase of reception and implementation.[2] If Kasper's third phase of reception and implementation is to be ongoing, then it demands a fresh appreciation of tradition in both Imbelli's aspects. It is the hope of this chapter to contribute to that fresh appreciation by examining the Eucharist in some of the conciliar and post-conciliar documents and by exploring the position of the Flemish Dominican Edward Schillebeeckx in his book *The Eucharist,* published in English three years after the Council.

The conciliar and post-conciliar documents

Sacrosanctum Concilium (The Constitution on the Sacred Liturgy), issued on 4 December 1963, was the first of the documents of the Council. Although from the point of view of a sacramental theologian this may seem providentially appropriate, in fact it was because the constitution's pre-conciliar preparation was more adequate and satisfactory than that of other texts.[3]

The first part of paragraph 7 reads as follows:

> To accomplish so great a work [of redemption] Christ is always present in his church, especially in [its] liturgical celebrations. He is present in the sacrifice of the Mass not only in the person of his minister, 'the same now offering, through the ministry of priests, who formerly offered himself on the cross', but especially in the eucharistic species. By his power he is present in the sacraments so that when anybody baptises it is really Christ himself who baptises. He is present in his word since it is he himself who speaks when the holy Scriptures are read in the

church. Lastly, he is present when the church prays and sings, for he has promised 'where two or three are gathered together in my name there I am in the midst of them'.[4]

Eucharistic sacrifice and eucharistic presence are both affirmed in this paragraph.

With regard to sacrifice, the statement follows tradition and quotes the Council of Trent, Session 22, 'Doctrine on the Holy Sacrifice of the Mass,' chapter 2. In paragraph 47 of the document, further comment is made on the eucharistic sacrifice: '[Christ instituted the eucharistic sacrifice] in order to perpetuate the sacrifice of the cross throughout the ages until he should come again, and so to entrust to his beloved spouse, the Church, a memorial of his death and resurrection…'.[5] In the discussion of the continuation of the sacrifice of Calvary, the concept of memorial is given emphasis.

This careful use of memorial to make the connection between the unique sacrifice of Christ and the celebration of the Eucharist reaches out with sensitivity to aspects of eucharistic theology in the Reformed tradition and is consonant with the same usage in such contemporary ecumenical statements as the World Council of Churches' *Baptism, Eucharist, Ministry* ('The Lima Statement') and the Anglican-Roman Catholic International Commission's *Windsor Report on the Eucharist.* In fact, in a magisterial article on sacrificial terminology and the Eucharist, Jean Tillard sees 'memorial' as the key to the various usages of Vatican Council II:

> In all the major liturgical documents and doctrinal texts connected with Vatican II the terms *perpetuare… representare:* and *praesens efficere…* are the 'official' terms by which Catholic faith in this field are expressed. Is it not possible to recognise here the vocabulary of the theology of *memorial?*[6]

With respect to eucharistic presence, in paragraph 7 of *Sacrosanctum Concilium* various modes of Christ's presence are noted – the minister, the eucharistic species, the word, the assembly – and the footnotes indicate here a retrieval of scriptural and patristic sources.

Eucharisticum Mysterium (Instruction on the Worship of the Eucharistic Mystery), 25 May 1967, summarises the conciliar eucharistic teaching, especially eucharistic presence, and offers further clarification:

> He is always present in a body of the faithful gathered in his name (cf. Matthew 18:20). He is present, too, in his word, for it is he who speaks when the Scriptures are read in the church. In the sacrifice of the Eucharist he is present both in the person of the minister, 'the same now offering through the ministry of the priest who formerly offered himself on the cross, and above all under the species of the Eucharist. For in this sacrament Christ is present in a unique way, whole and entire, God and man, substantially and permanently. The presence of Christ under the species is called 'real' not in an exclusive sense, as if the other kinds of presence were not real, but *par excellence.*[7]

Some were not altogether happy about the use of the term *par excellence* to distinguish the mode of Christ's presence in the eucharistic species from the other modes. It seems to some to diminish the presence of Christ in the eucharistic species. How is one to respond to this concern? The total context establishes that there is no desire to reduce or diminish the presence of Christ in the eucharistic species. But perhaps the teaching office of the Church is trying to highlight a more fully ecclesial understanding of Christ's presence for Catholics, more in harmony with the tradition, and to move Catholics on from an *exclusive* focus on the eucharistic species. This would appear to be the case especially when one takes into account Section F of the same document, where we read:

> Thus the Church is nourished by the bread of life which [it] finds at the table both of the word of God and of the body of Christ.[8]

Edward Schillebeeckx (b. 1914)

Edward Schillebeeckx, the Flemish Dominican theologian, accompanied the Dutch bishops to the Council as their theological adviser. Schillebeeckx's doctoral dissertation had been a patristic and medieval study of the sacraments. This study appeared in Dutch in 1952, and though it has never been translated into English, a non-technical summary may be found in his *Christ the Sacrament of the Encounter With God*, published in 1963. Sacramental theology is a major preoccupation of the early Schillebeeckx, and it is to his *The Eucharist* that we now turn to exemplify an important strand of eucharistic theology contemporary with and consequent upon the Council.

The Eucharist was published in English in 1968, and it has become something of a classic. Various new approaches to the Eucharist, using contemporary philosophies and less dependent on neo-scholasticism, had been appearing in the Netherlands in theological and catechetical journals not readily accessible to the English-speaking world for over ten years. But it was largely Schillebeeckx's *The Eucharist* that brought these approaches to the attention of the English-speaking theological world.

The new approaches were found by some to be disturbing, even to be erosive of eucharistic faith, but Schillebeeckx's grasp of the tradition enabled him to speak with immediacy to this mindset:

> *Historia, magistra vitae!* A close look at the Christian past always brings profound claim to the life of faith in the midst of the fevered search for new interpretations. Our faith subsists in historicity.[9]

With his historically sensitive hermeneutic, Schillebeeckx turns his attention on to the Tridentine approach to Eucharist, but at the outset he notes that we have in the Eucharist 'one of the most delicate of all the living mysteries of the Catholic faith,' which must be handled with consummate care.[10]

At the Council of Trent, there was no discussion about the notion of 'change'/*conversio* in the Eucharist (this was simply taken as given), but there was discussion about the term 'transubstantiation'. Some bishops did not feel the term was appropriate because it was something of a 'newcomer' to the tradition, and yet the Council fathers as a whole were to conclude, 'Although the word [transubstantiation] is of more recent date, the real faith (*fides et res*) is none the less very old.'[11]

On the other hand, many bishops were of the view that 'transubstantiation' was to Trent what *homoousios* was to Nicaea, that is, while not a scriptural term, it was necessary to expose heresy. 'As such, the word itself explained nothing. It was simply intended as a kind of distinguishing mark by which the Christian could make his own position in the doctrine of the Eucharist immediately clear.'[12]

For the Tridentine fathers 'real presence' and 'transubstantiation' were identical affirmations. They were identical because the framework of thought of the fathers at Trent was Aristotelian philosophy so much so that they could not have done other than use this philosophy to express their Catholic sense of eucharistic presence. The Catholic sense of eucharistic presence at Trent is therefore continuous with that of the patristic period, but expressed in different terms at a different point in history. For the fathers of Trent as of the patristic period, the bread and wine in the celebration of the Eucharist acquired a radically new being, 'that of the body of Christ, the saving organ of the Logos'.[13]

For Schillebeeckx, the central question is 'What is reality?' He notes that there are differences between the Catholic and the Protestant views of reality, differences which make themselves felt in the fundamental themes of theology. The Catholic view of reality is this:

> The creature does not need to give way to God when he approaches, as water has to give way to a piece of wood that is plunged into it. On the contrary, the creature is completely permeated by God without any withdrawal whatever. God is not a fellow creature who occupies his own space beside and to whom I have to yield if he wants to occupy my space as well. He is, even when he confers grace, transcendent through interiority.[14]

In the Catholic perspective reality is not beyond God's presence, but rather mediates that presence. God is present in the communication of himself in grace to his creation, but this presence has 'an unexpectedly profound ontological density in this particular gift of himself in the Eucharist, since it takes hold of the secular reality of the bread creatively and is not simply a transcendent 'naming from outside' which leaves the secular reality as it was before…'[15] If you will, heaven comes to us mediately through the secular, the horizontal, and not immediately from the vertical. All of this forms the backdrop to Schillebeeckx's handling of eucharistic presence.

In developing a fresh approach to eucharistic presence, Schillebeeckx starts from anthropology and not from the philosophy of nature (substance/transubstantiation). This new approach did not occur in a vacuum, but had been heralded by a series of phenomena that had an impact on theology. First is the conflict between an Aristotelian concept of reality and modern physics. Modern physics had shaken the speculations of neo-scholasticism about the concept of substance 'to their foundations'. Second is the rediscovery of the sacramental-symbolic approach in contrast to a 'physical approach' to the Eucharist, the notion that *sacramentum est in genere signi*, and here Schillebeeckx notes the important role played by Anscar Vonier.[16] Third is the more nuanced hermeneutical approach to the Tridentine concept of substance, and the distance between Aristotelian categories and modern philosophical thought. Fourth is the manifold realisation of the 'real presence' of Christ expressed in *Sacrosanctum Concilium* and *Mysterium Fidei*. Fifth is the desire for Christian unity, and Schillebeeckx shows himself appreciative of the work of theologians such as Max Thurian (now Catholic) and F. J. Leenhardt. In his judgement, these are the most important factors stimulating a new approach to the Eucharist.

The fundament for Schillebeeckx's new approach to eucharistic presence is the believer's recognition that creation, as God's pure and gratuitous communication of himself, establishes a personal presence of God in all things. 'In this sense, it is therefore possible to say that the entire world has a general quasi-sacramental significance.'[17] This fundamental recognition has at least one major consequence, that although man gives meaning to reality, the meanings given by man 'are governed by a reality which is... in the first place God's, and only then man's'.[18] The person's giving meaning to reality, giving 'signification' to reality, is his humanising the world, or his living 'from continuous transsignifications.'[19] It is an account of *being* as *meaning*. Because of this a thing can become essentially different without being biologically or physically changed. Thus, an animal's eating is essentially different from human eating, because people give meaning to the action.

Using the work of Bernhard Welte, Schillebeeckx illustrates being as meaning with two fine examples, a Greek temple and a national flag. 'A Greek temple is something different for its builders, for those who worship in it and for modern tourists. Man himself is essentially involved in this change of relationship, but it is not completely dependent on him – the being itself of things changes when the relationship is altered... a coloured cloth is purely decorative, but if a government decides to raise it to the level of a national flag, then the same cloth is really and objectively no longer the same. Physically nothing has been changed, but its being is essentially changed.'[20]

In the liturgy the significance given to bread means that is *is not* bread, but the very presence of Christ, Christ's gift of himself. The usual, mundane significance of bread and wine in this context is withdrawn, and they become the bearers of Christ's gift of himself. Transsignification has occurred. A new ontology is established. This significance is not subjective, that is, it is not given by the individual believer to the bread and wine. Rather, this new significance is established by Jesus Christ: 'Take and eat, this is my body…,' not in the sense of a historical religious figure, but in the sense of the living Lord *in* the Church. Through his living presence in the definitive community of salvation that is the Church, this 'establishment of meaning' is given to the bread and wine so that they *are* the very gift of himself. This giving of meaning is accomplished from the Lord in the Church, or from the Church as living in the Lord. For Schillebeeckx, to separate absolutely Christ and the Church is to make a category mistake.

Conclusion

In both the conciliar and post-conciliar documents, and in the work of theologians like Edward Schillebeeckx, we see Imbelli's two aspects of tradition. Both, on the one hand, retrieve the broad horizon of Catholic eucharistic reflection and doctrine; and equally, on the other hand, both try to interpret that tradition in ways that will render it intelligible and fruitful for the contemporary Church. Some may point to Pope Paul VI's remarks in *Mysterium Fidei* as being opposed to such theories as transsignification, but a careful reading will yield no global condemnation of the theory but rather a proper regard to protect the substance of the eucharistic faith. It is not fanciful to see in the official ecclesial documents and in the theological work of such as Schillebeeckx the 'double magisterium' of the teaching office of the Church and of its theologians at its creative best.

6

THE EUCHARIST AND POPE JOHN PAUL II

It may be that, given the truth in the axiom *lex orandi statuat legem credendi*, the most significant aspect of Pope John Paul II's eucharistic theology is, in fact, his celebration of the Eucharist among the people of the world during his many travels. As the Bishop of Rome, sacrament of the church's unity, he breaks bread and shares the cup with local churches, thus expressing both the unity and the catholicity of the Church.

Nevertheless, Pope John Paul has issued one important statement on the Eucharist, *Dominicae Cenae* (On The Mystery and Worship of the Most Holy Eucharist) in 1980, and to this we now turn our attention. Aidan Nichols describes it as 'a miniature compendium of the doctrinal development' of the Eucharist, and Edward Kilmartin considers it 'one of the more significant papal contributions to the theology of the Eucharist in the twentieth century'.[1]

Analysis of *Dominicae Cenae*

From the viewpoint of literary genre, *Dominicae Cenae* is an *epistula*, a circular letter sent to the whole episcopal college.[2] It is divided into three parts: the eucharistic mystery in the life of the Church and of the priest; the sacred character of the Eucharist and the sacrifice; the two tables of the Lord and the common possession of the Church.

In the first section, the pope stresses the intimate link between the Eucharist and the sacrament of the priesthood:

> The Eucharist is the principal and central *raison d'être* of the sacrament of the priesthood.... We are united in a singular and exceptional way to the Eucharist. In a certain way we derive from it and exist for it'. (§2. p.71)

This particular emphasis in the *epistula* is valuable in at least this respect, that it underscores the essential link between the priest and the Eucharist – not only in his presidential function but also in terms of his spiritual life – and provides clear direction at a time when there is some confusion about the role of the priest in society. At the same time, the pope goes on to comment on the absolutely central significance of the Eucharist for the entire Church.

The celebration of the Eucharist and ongoing eucharistic devotion adumbrate the traditional axiom that 'the Church makes the Eucharist and the Eucharist builds up the Church' (§4, p.73). The union and communion that is the Church is brought into being not only through the experience of brotherhood, but also through the sacramental nourishment of receiving holy communion. The Eucharist, therefore, may be said to constitute 'the soul of all Christian life' (§5, p.75).

As the animating principle of the Church, the Eucharist leads to a particular perception and transformation of human relationships:

> If our eucharistic worship is authentic, it must make us grow in awareness of the dignity of each person. The awareness of that dignity becomes the deepest motives of our relationship with our neighbour. We must also become particularly sensitive to all human suffering and misery, to all injustice and wrong, and seek the way to redress them effectively (§6, p.76).

This particular focus of the letter speaks clearly to the contemporary interest, especially of liberation theologians, in establishing links between the Eucharist and the promotion of justice in the world, to the topic for consideration in chapter 8 below.

In the second section of the letter, the papal concern is with the sacrificial dimension of the Eucharist:

> The Eucharist is above all else a sacrifice (§9, p.81).

The eucharistic sacrifice, sacramentally representing the unique sacrifice of Christ on the cross, restores humankind and the world to God. This is brought about by the agency of the ordained priest, and in consent with him, by virtue of the common priesthood '[the faithful] offer with him their own spiritual sacrifices represented by the bread and wine' (§9, p.81). Thus, the entire liturgical assembly, but as an *ordered* assembly, participates in the sacramental sacrifice.

A *lacuna* here seems to be that there is little awareness of the meaning and nature of sacrifice as this has emerged in ecumenical dialogue about the Eucharist, although to be fair this is 'not simply a doctrinal treatise on the Eucharist,'[3] and we should not expect to find systematic coverage of eucharistic doctrine.

In the third section, the pope uses the patristic reference to the two tables of the word of God and the Eucharist. He emphasises the importance of the Liturgy of the Word and offers a reminder that the readings from Scripture cannot be replaced by the reading of other texts, however valuable. At the same time, however, he notes that 'such texts can be used very profitably in the homily' (§10, p.85).

Concluding his commentary on *Dominicae Cenae,* Edward Kilmartin has this to say:

> The pope is above all concerned with deepening the unity of the Catholic Church and with resolving tensions which exist in the Church due to the post-conciliar liturgical renewal. Hence the choice of subjects is influenced by the objections of reactionary groups to changes in the liturgy. The mode of argumentation is also probably determined

in great part by the desire to speak to 'Tridentine' Catholics within their frame of reference.[4]

Kilmartin's judgement is accurate. While earlier twentieth century popes (Pius X, Pius XII) were concerned, as we have seen in chapter 4 above, with rendering the Eucharist accessible to people, Pope John Paul II is concerned in this document with deepening the unity of the Church in the wake of conflict consequent upon the liturgical revisions of the Second Vatican Council.

The Lima Statement

Two other documents with significant eucharistic content have emerged during the pontificate of Pope John Paul II: the section on the Eucharist in the so-called 'Lima statement' on Baptism, *Eucharist and Ministry* of the World Council of Churches,[5] and the section on the Eucharist in *Catechism of the Catholic Church*.[6] An examination and contrast of these two documents will show a reasonable degree of convergence on the Eucharist.

The opening paragraph of the Lima Statement links the Eucharist to its Old Testament roots:

> Christians see the Eucharist prefigured in the Passover memorial of Israel's deliverance from the land of bondage and the meal of the covenant on Mount Sinai (Ex 24). It is the new paschal meal of the Church, the meal of the new covenant, which Christ gave to his disciples as the *anamnesis* of his death and resurrection, as the anticipation of the supper of the Lamb. (Rv 19:9)[7]

The key emphasis immediately is on the notion of *anamnesis*/memorial. Just as the Passover meal recalls-through-making-present the unique liberating experience of the Exodus, the Eucharist, as the paschal meal of Christ-in-the-Church, performs a similar function for the people of the new covenant. The eschatological note is also welcome, linking the Eucharist with the heavenly banquet.

The statement then proceeds to treat of the Eucharist under the following headings: thanksgiving to the Father, memorial of Christ, invocation of the Spirit, communion of the faithful, meal of the kingdom. It is most pleasing to find a strong Trinitarian aspect to the eucharistic theology of the Lima Statement, especially when one considers the marginalising of the doctrine of the Trinity that was a consequence of the (at least cryto-) unitarianism of such liberal English language works as Geoffrey Lampe's *God As Spirit* (Oxford: The Clarendon Press, 1977), and John Hick's symposium *The Myth of God Incarnate* (London: SCM Press, 1977).

The Eucharist is the great thanksgiving to the Father for creation, redemption, and sanctification. 'The Eucharist is the great sacrifice of praise by which the Church speaks on behalf of the whole creation.'[8] This is an aspect of the eucharistic theology that is deeply patristic and resonates with the great tradition of the Orthodox Churches.

As the memorial of Christ, the Eucharist is 'the living and effective sign of his sacrifice, accomplished once and for all on the cross and still operative on behalf on all humankind'.[9]

Care is taken here to acknowledge particularly the sensitivities about the sacrifice of Christ in Reformed eucharistic theologies. The *ephapax* of the sacrifice in the Letter to the Hebrews is expressed unambiguously, but at the same time, is living, effective, and still operative. The form of expression may not be common for Catholics, but the sentiments are truly Catholic.

At the same time, the Eucharist is 'the sacrament of the body and blood of Christ, the sacrament of his real presence. Christ fulfils in a variety of ways his promise to be always with his own to the end of the world. But Christ's mode of presence in the Eucharist is unique.'[10] A Catholic could not fail to recognise in this affirmation a strong family resemblance to paragraph 7 of *Sacrosanctum Concilium* and *Eucharisticum Mysterium.*

Finally, in Trinitarian terms, the Eucharist is the invocation of the Holy Spirit:

> The bond between the eucharistic celebration and the mystery of the Triune God reveals the role of the Holy Spirit as that of the one who makes the historical word of Jesus present and alive.[11]

The epiclesis in eucharistic theology has always been a characteristic of the Orthodox tradition, but with the creation of new eucharistic prayers it has been retrieved by Catholics.

The Eucharist is also the communion of the faithful and the meal of the kingdom. 'Eucharistic communion with Christ is at the same time communion within the body of Christ which is the Church…. It is in the Eucharist that the community of God's people is fully manifested… All kinds of injustice, racism, separation and lack of freedom are radically challenged when we share in the body and blood of Christ.'[12]

Going no further than *Dominicae Cenae* we can see clear and central Catholic concerns reflected here: the mutual efficient causality between the Church and the Eucharist and the intrinsic connection with social justice. This latter point is given yet further emphasis when the Eucharist is seen as the proleptic meal of the kingdom. Since the kingdom of God is not just something individualistic and personal but is social and communal and subversive of 'worldly' values, the Eucharist as the anticipatory kingdom meal gives further impetus to the achievement of social justice.

The Catechism

The Catechism of the Catholic Church is undoubtedly one of the highlights of the pontificate of Pope John Paul II. Coming some twenty-five years after the close of the Second Vatican Council, the *Catechism* is probably best understood as a 'manual of Catholic grammar', providing a route towards the establishment of basic Catholic literacy in matters of faith. The *Catechism* is divided essentially into four sections, well described by many as the 'four pillars' of the *Catechism*: the creed, the sacraments, morality, prayer. Berard Marthaler develops this architectural model of the *Catechism*: 'The image of structuring the catechism on the 'four pillars' of catechesis conjures up a picture of a Roman *palazzo* built in the Renaissance and modernised after the Second World War. The façade and the foundations remain unchanged,but the interior has been remodelled. So it is with the *Catechism of the Catholic Church*: old and new at the same time.'[13] Within this four-pillared structure of the *Catechism* there is a most useful apparatus that enables cross-referral throughout the text, and so reference to the Eucharist may be found in a variety of places. However, the central treatment of the Eucharist comes in the section devoted to the sacraments.

What one notices immediately through these eucharistic categories is the Trinitarian movement of the *Catechism's* eucharistic theology. First, praise and thanksgiving to the Father for all that God has done in creation. Through the Eucharist, the Church '...sings the glory of God in the name of all creation' (§ 1361). The Church consciously represents the entire cosmos in acknowledging the sovereignty of God in its paean of praise to the Creator. A passage from the late Orthodox liturgical theologian, Alexander Schmemann, provides a helpful comment on this point.

> It is the natural sacramentality of the world that finds its expression in worship.... Being the epiphany of God, worship is thus the epiphany of the world; being communion with God, it is the only true communion with the world; being knowledge of God, it is the ultimate fulfilment of all human knowledge.[14]

The human person has an obligation (moral and religious) to hymn God's praise on behalf of all creation.

Second is the sacrificial memorial of Christ and his body, the Church. The Eucharist is the *memorial* of Christ's passover, making present sacramentally his unique sacrifice on Calvary (§1362). Because the Church is the body of Christ, the Eucharist is 'equally the Church's sacrifice' (§1368). The Church participates in the offering of Christ, its head. Nor is this liturgical rhetoric. The *Catechism* goes on to specify just what this means in terms of the members of the Church; 'In the Eucharist, the sacrifice of Christ becomes also the sacrifice of the members of his body. The lives of the faithful, their praise, sufferings, prayers and work, are united with those of Christ and with his total offering and so acquire a new value. Christ's sacrifice, present on the altar, makes it possible for all generations of Christians to be united with his offering' (§1368). It may be that the Eucharist provides all the elements of a Catholic theodicy in which response to the problem of evil and suffering is not first analytical and theoretical, but liturgical and doxological.[15]

This approach to the sacrifice of Christ eschews any doctrinal or liturgical extrinsicism, notionally 'out there' to be accepted and appropriated by the faithful. On the contrary, as the body of Christ, the faithful are living out ontologically the meaning of that identity by articulating in the context of their lives the individual, social and ethical consequences of their ecclesial union with the Lord.

The *Catechism* summarises this powerful notion in a quotation from Augustine's *City of God* (10:6):

> This wholly redeemed city, the assembly and society of the saints, is offered to God as a universal sacrifice by the high priest who in the form of a slave went so far as to offer himself for us in his Passion, to make us the Body of so great a head... Such is the sacrifice of Christians: 'we who

are many are one Body in Christ.' The Church continues to reproduce this sacrifice in the sacrament of the altar so well-known to believers wherein it is evident to them that in what she offers she herself is offered. (§1372)

Third, Christ is present by the power of his word and the Holy Spirit. As would be expected in a document reflecting the teachings of the Council, there is a clear appreciation of the various modes of Christ's presence, as expressed in *Sacrosanctum Concilium* (§7): in his word, in the Church's prayer, in the poor, sick and imprisoned, in the sacraments, in the Mass, and in the person of his minister. Christ is 'present most especially in the eucharistic species' (§1373).

This latter mode of Christ's presence demonstrates the Eucharist as 'the perfection of the spiritual life and the end to which all the sacraments tend' (§1374). The centrality and importance of Christ's eucharistic presence for the health of the spiritual life is further underscored in the document by a quotation from paragraph 3 of *Dominicae Cenae*:

'The Church and the world have a great need for eucharistic worship. Jesus awaits us in this sacrament of love. Let us not refuse the time to go out to meet him in adoration, in contemplation full of faith and open to making amends for the serious offenses and crimes of the world. Let our adoration never cease'. (§1380)

The final item within this section to which attention should be drawn has to do with the Eucharist and justice. 'The Eucharist commits us to the poor. To receive in truth the Body and Blood of Christ given up for us, we must recognise Christ in the poorest, his brethren' (§1397). The vertical and the horizontal aspects of eucharistic worship are thus held in a fine balance.

Conclusion

There is a high, positive correlation between the theology of the Eucharist found in the Lima Statement and in the *Catechism of the Catholic Church*. Both seem to agree in at least the following ways: a Trinitarian structure for an adequate appreciation of the meaning of the Eucharist; the Eucharist as thanksgiving to the Father for creation; the Eucharist as the *anamnesis*/memorial of Christ's unique and unrepeatable sacrifice on the cross; the various modes of Christ's eucharistic presence, climaxing in the eucharistic elements themselves; the connection between the Eucharist and the promotion of justice in the world.

Eucharistic theology during the pontificate of Pope John Paul II seems, then, to have two foci: deepening the unity of the Church in the wake of conciliar renewal and an ecumenical awareness of the richness and breadth of the eucharistic tradition. And here lies our best clue as to the future of eucharistic theology.

It is difficult to envisage any future development that would move behind these two foci just noted. It is safe to say that no eucharistic renewal or development is conceivable that is not first established on a fruitful retrieval of the past. And equally, it is safe to maintain that the ear of what might be called 'classical ecumenism' is over. Christian unity is best served not by blueprints for institutional merger, but through prayerful, informed growing together. To adapt a phrase of Avery Dulles, the future of eucharistic theology seems to lie in heterogeneous eucharistic communities of witnessing dialogue.[16]

THE EUCHARISTIC PRESENCE OF CHRIST

In December 1991 and January 1992, a Gallup poll was taken on American understanding of the Eucharist. The findings of the poll leave something to be desired, to say the least. Though I have not been privy to the complete sociological apparatus of the poll, the Catholic press has carried the following facts and figures. Of the Catholics interviewed, 29 per cent think they 'are receiving bread and wine, which symbolise the spirit and teachings of Jesus and in so doing are expressing [their] attachment to his person and words'; 10 per cent understand that they 'are receiving bread and wine, in which Jesus is really and truly present'; 23 per cent believe they 'are receiving the body and blood of Christ which has become that because of [their] personal belief'; and only 30 per cent believe that they 'are really and truly receiving the body and blood, soul and divinity of the Lord Jesus Christ, under the appearances of bread and wine'.

It seems to me that difficult hermeneutical issues arise in exploring doctrinal understanding through a poll. For example: What precisely did the subjects understand that they were being asked? Who composed the questions? In what order did they come, and why? One of the most serious hermeneutical issues is how doctrinal orthodoxy is to be measured. Is it measured through conceptual clarity and articulateness, or how it is expressed in the lives of believers? Many devout Catholics, I suspect, would not be able to give a precise, coherent resumé of many aspects of Catholic faith, and yet their daily Christian living indicates how well such doctrine has been appropriated.

Nonetheless, it is fair to say on the basis of the poll that there seems to be a measure of confusion among Catholics about the eucharistic presence of Christ. The purpose of this chapter is to address that confusion by unpacking the principal elements of

Catholic teaching on this issue, but before attempting to do so, I wish to make my own some words of Karl Rahner in an essay written on this topic in 1957:

> I am concerned to say, right from the start, that I do not consider it the task and the duty of a Catholic theologian to act as it everything were perfectly clear, as if the firmness of his assent to the doctrine of his Church depended on his having the answers to all questions.[1]

Rahner is not avoiding the proper and legitimate quest for clarity in doctrinal issues. Rather, he is explicitly acknowledging the insight of the First Vatican Council that 'if reason illuminated by faith inquires in an earnest, pious and sober manner, it attains by God's grace a *certain* understanding of the mysteries...'.[2] 'A certain understanding' is not a complete understanding. Indeed, to maintain that one had a complete understanding of the mysteries/doctrines of the faith would seem to be blasphemous. Before articulating a certain understanding, then, of eucharistic presence, it is useful to indicate that there was no 'golden age' of eucharistic action and reflection, free of difficulties and problems.

No 'Golden Age'
Every generation the Church experiences its own difficulties and crises. But there is a tendency to think of the current crisis as more serious than anything before. This could well be true of an individual period in Church history with regard to a specific issue. However, even a brief historical perspective may indicate that this is not necessarily the case. Let me attend to two problems at different times in the history of eucharistic action and reflection.

The first problems comes from the earliest account of the Eucharist that we possess, 1 Corinthians 11:17-30. Around the year 56, Paul wrote to the Christian community in Corinth about a troublesome matter to do with the eucharistic celebration. At the time, the Eucharist was celebrated in someone's home in the context of a community meal. Paul writes to the Corinthians:

> When you meet in one place, then, it is not to eat the Lord's supper, for in eating, each one goes ahead with his own supper, and goes hungry while another gets drunk.[3]

He upbraids the Corinthians for being self-indulgent at the Lord's supper in such a way that they evacuate the Lord's supper of genuine meaning. They eat and drink 'without discerning the body', that is, the community of believers.

The second problem is found in the church of North Africa, in Cyprian's *Letter 63*, which has been discussed at greater length in chapter 1. The date seems to be around 254-256 and the problem is that some Christians are not using wine for the celebration of the Eucharist. At this time, Christianity has not yet been recognised under Roman law as a *religio licita*, and therefore, it is strictly illegal. Some Christians, to avoid detection and the possibility of persecution, are using only bread in the celebration of the Eucharist. Cyprian writes to them:

> It may be that some feel apprehensive at our morning sacrifices that if they taste wine they may exhale the smell of the blood of Christ. That is the sort of thinking which causes our brethren to become reluctant to share even in Christ's sufferings in times of persecution, by thus learning in making their oblation to be ashamed of the blood that Christ has shed himself.[4]

In Cyprian's thinking such Christians devalue both the Eucharist and the quality of their own Christian witness.

Even in this early period, so close to the origins of Christian faith, there were problems with the Eucharist. Historians of doctrine could multiply such examples, but these will suffice to indicate that there never was a 'golden age'.

From Trent to the Second Vatican Council

The basic grammar of Catholic belief in the eucharistic presence of Christ derives from two councils of the Church, Trent and the Second Vatican. Two decrees of the Council of Trent deal with the Eucharist: *The Decree On the Most Holy Eucharist,* from the thirteenth session in 1551, and *The Doctrine On The Most Holy Sacrifice,* from the twenty-second session in 1562. Our concern is with the former.

The intention of the Council fathers, as described in the foreword, is 'to set forth the true and ancient doctrine on the faith and on the sacraments…'. And it ends: 'The council forbids all the faithful of Christ henceforth to believe, teach or preach anything about the most Holy Eucharist that is different from what is explained and defined in the present decree.'[5] The Council fathers, therefore, were not out to develop eucharistic doctrine in some new way, but simply to state 'the ancient doctrine' of the Church against what were perceived to be the errors of the reformers, Luther, Calvin and Zwingli. Rahner comments:

> They merely repeated, as it was itself the right thing to do, what the Church had already been saying for many hundreds of years before them when such discussion arose in the same explicit formulas.[6]

Chapter 1 of the Decree is entitled: 'The Real Presence of Our Lord Jesus Christ in the Most Holy Sacrament of the Eucharist'. Consistent with the Western approach to the Eucharist, the Council affirms that 'after the consecration of the bread and wine, our Lord Jesus Christ, true God and Man, is truly, really and substantially contained under the appearances of those perceptible realities'. The text continues by insisting that there is no contradiction between the fact of Christ's sitting at the right hand of the Father in heaven, and that 'in his substance he is sacramentally present to us in many other places. We can hardly find words to express this way of existing; but our reason, enlightened through faith, can nevertheless recognise it as possible for God, and we must always believe it unhesitatingly.'[7]

Oftentimes, the teachings of Trent are interpreted as being myopic, but a balanced reading of the decrees, within the total fabric of doctrine, reveals otherwise.[8] Two things are particularly striking about this aforementioned passage. First, the acknowledgment that Christ is 'sacramentally present to us in many other places'. The focus of the fathers is no denial of Christ's presence being sacramentally witnessed elsewhere. Second, the council fathers admit the difficulty of putting their belief in Christ's presence into a form of words: '…we can hardly find words to express this way of existing'. No eucharistic rationalism here, but rather, what we might call a reverence before the mystery.

In chapter 2 of the decree, 'The Reason for the Institution of this Most Holy Sacrament', we read that Christ instituted the 'Eucharist… causing his wonderful works to be remembered… and he wanted us when receiving it to celebrate his memory'.[9] Later eucharistic theology will make much of the concept of 'memorial', especially drawing upon its ecumenical potential, as we have seen in the last chapter.

It is surely interesting to see this idea of 'memorial' used by the Tridentine fathers.[10] Christ willed that the Eucharist be 'a symbol of that one "body" of which he himself is "the head".[11] What Aidan Nichols terms 'the ecclesial rationale' for the real presence is given expression here. Medieval eucharistic theology, which is essentially being received by Trent, has as one of its rationale for the real presence of Christ in the Eucharist the uniting of

Christian believers to each other through their union with Christ. Nichols nicely refers to this as 'the perichoresis or mutual indwelling' of Church and Eucharist.[12]

'Transubstantiation' comes up for treatment in chapter 4 of the decree:

> It has always been the conviction of the Church of God, and this holy council now again declares that, by the consecration of the bread and wine there takes place a change of the whole substance of bread into the substance of the body of Christ our Lord and of the whole substance of wine into the substance of his blood. This change the holy Catholic Church has fittingly (*convenienter*) and properly (*proprie*) named transubstantiation.[13]

In using this term, the council, true to its intention of doing nothing but retrieving the tradition, is citing the Fourth Lateran Council in 1215, which is the first occasion on which a Church council uses the term 'transubstantiation'. The bread is changed into the body of Christ and the wine into his bread, and the council adds that this is 'fittingly' and 'properly' named 'transubstantiation'.

Three points may be made by way of clarification. First, in using this term in harmony with the Fourth Lateran Council, the Council fathers intend nothing more, but nothing less, than what we might call 'the plain sense' of the Scriptures. Karl Rahner puts it like this:

> The doctrine of transubstantiation tells me no more than do the words of Christ, when I take them seriously. The function of this doctrine is not to explain the real presence by accounting for *how* it takes place... It is a way of formulating the truth *that* the body is present.[14]

Second, it is not intended to be a rational explanation of the mystery of the Eucharist which can be grasped only in faith. Third, because the mystery is grasped only in faith, the eucharistic presence of Christ is not connected to the domain of what is accessible to natural-scientific investigation. At the level of sense experience, the eucharistic gifts do not change in terms of smell, taste and chemical composition.[15] The eucharistic change cannot be 'proved' or 'verified', but only approved and accepted through the ecclesial faith by the faithful Christian. Ultimately, the traditional claim of Trent is that 'substance' means the 'radical reality of a thing, as opposed to what a thing appears to be'.[16] The real merit of transubstantiation is to affirm that the eucharistic presence of Christ is real, not to define anything rashly about the method of the presence.[17]

The key passage in the documents of the Second Vatican Council relating to the eucharistic presence, as has been noted in chapter 5, comes in *The Constitution On the Sacred Liturgy* (§7):

> To accomplish so great a work [of redemption] Christ is always present in his Church, especially in [its] liturgical celebrations. He is present in the sacrifice of the Mass not only in the person of his minister... but especially in the eucharistic species. By his power he is present in the sacraments so that when anybody baptises it is really Christ himself who baptises. He is present in his word since it is he himself who speaks when the Holy Scriptures are read in the church. Lastly, he is present when the church prays and sings, for he has promised 'where two or three are gathered together in my name there am I in the midst of them'.

There are two important points to note about this statement. First and fundamental is the affirmation of Christ's presence in the Church, and especially in liturgical celebrations. Secondly, with regard to the sacrifice of the mass, the affirmation indicates four modes of Christ's presence. In the sequence of the statement they are: in the presiding priest, in the eucharistic species, in the assembly, in the proclamation of the word. The conciliar text also provides the reason for Christ's presence among us – to associate us in his great work of redemption.

In 1967 the Sacred Congregation of Rites published *Eucharisticum Mysterium* (The Instruction on the Worship of the Eucharistic Mystery), in which these issues are further clarified. In Section E of the document, after reiterating the modes of Christ's eucharistic presence from the Constitution on the Liturgy, we read 'that the presence of Christ in the eucharistic species is called "real", not as though the other modes of presence were somehow unreal, but *par excellence*'. The statement introduces nothing particularly new. It is a synthesis drawing upon both Trent and Vatican II, and the words of Pope Paul VI in his encyclical letter *Mysterium Fidei* (1965).

We might also note in this context that part of the rationale for the recent change in the conclusion to the readings in the Liturgy of the Word from 'This is the word of the Lord' to 'The word of the Lord' is to maintain the parallel to the distribution formula for Communion, 'The body of Christ'. What the Vatican Council and the subsequent documentation has achieved is in no sense a corrective to the Tridentine decree, but a retrieval of a richer and ultimately more traditional approach to the question of the eucharistic presence.

There are three further questions that might be raised to aid our understanding. The first question is: When do the eucharistic gifts become the body and blood of Christ? 'The Church teaches that the true and real presence of Jesus Christ in the forms of bread and wine is secured by the words of Jesus: "This is my body," "This is my blood".[18] Lest this be understood in too mechanical a fashion, it should be noted that these dominical words do not stand in isolation but are irreducibly part of the fabric of the entire eucharistic prayer. They cannot be understood liturgically apart from the enabling context of the eucharistic prayer. In that sense, the entire eucharistic prayer is the context that effects the change, the dominical words of institution being the climax of the prayer. At the same time, it seems to me that we need to move away – in view of the manifold presence of Christ – from an invasive model of Christ's presence. Sometimes, in popular parlance, the presence of Christ in the Eucharist is spoken of as though he were otherwise normally absent. To help us reflect on a non-invasive model of Christ's presence, the expression of the Anglican systematic theologian, Timothy Gorringe, is particularly helpful:

> God engages: the reason there is anything rather than nothing. The symbol of the Trinity is the attempt to articulate what it means to live within that continuing engagement. Sacramental language developed and continues to develop, to point up the occasions, events, moments, situations where lesions in the absorption of everyday reveal the mystery of this inventive and subversive engagement.[19]

The Eucharist, as the most perfect 'lesion in the absorption of everyday', reveals and manifests in a unique way the presence that is never absent. Furthermore, Gorringe's formulation helps us to recover the more properly Trinitarian dimension. 'Jesus Christ's becoming present in the Eucharist is not something magical or mechanical. It takes place through a *prayer* directed to God, the Father, in the name of Jesus Christ *for the gift of the Holy Spirit*.'[20]

   The second question is: How does the 'real presence' of Christ in the eucharistic gifts differ from his no less real presence in the Christian community, in the word, in the other sacraments, in other 'lesions in the absorption of everyday'? Obviously, it is a qualitative rather than an absolute difference, a matter of intensity rather than of kind. There is simply no other way of putting it because all 'sacramental reality is always the enduring reality of the incarnate God'.[21] The presence of Christ in the eucharistic gifts is the climactic realisation, known in faith, of God in Christ by the power of the Holy Spirit.[22]

The third question: Is this real presence of Christ in the eucharistic gifts permanent? The Catholic answer is in the affirmative, and the fundaments of that answer are to be found in Trent's 1551 *Decree on The Most Holy Eucharist*. Chapter 2 of the Decree insists that the Eucharist comes from the Lord to be received and to be eaten by the faithful.[23] Again, in canon 4 at the end of the Decree there is the insistence that Christ is present in the gifts not only while they are being received in communion, but also in the consecrated hosts that remain over. The one truth is ordered to the other. Rahner puts it well:

> Clearly as the council rejects the doctrine that Christ is only present '*in usu, dum sumitur*', it concedes just as readily that this sacrament was instituted by Christ '*ut sumitur*'.... The more clearly, therefore, the reverent adoration of Christ in the sacrament is referred back to the eating of the body of Christ, the more eucharistic piety corresponds to the full truth and reality of the sacrament.[24]

Just as the assembly remains the mystical body of Christ between celebrations of the Eucharist, so, once bread has been consecrated, it does not cease to be the eucharistic body of Christ. It is always standing by, so to speak, 'to be used in the Christian assembly – whether for communicating the sick and other absent members, or as a focus of praise and adoration by people grateful for the last celebration of the Eucharist and looking forward to the next one'.[25]

Cultivating a eucharistic sensibility
If this rich nexus of understanding the eucharistic presence of

Christ is to be appropriated by the faithful, then there is an obvious psychological need for mediative eucharistic prayer, a need that cannot be met during the brief duration of the Mass itself. 'The Mass must be prepared in prayer, prolonged in prayer, if it is to be for us authentically the Mass.'[26] This indicates the importance of traditional eucharistic devotions.

These devotions – benediction, holy hours, private prayer before the Blessed Sacrament – are simply ways of appropriating the meaning of the Eucharist, and through this conscious appropriation, of renewing our self-understanding in both identity and mission as the Body of Christ. Cahal Daly comments beautifully:

> Prayer before the blessed Sacrament cannot but be marked with this twofold passion, to sanctify and to spread the Church and to transform and Christify and eucharistify the earth.[27]

Conclusion

This essay had as its aim to unpack the principal elements of Catholic teaching about the eucharistic presence of Christ. Other important aspects of eucharistic doctrine need also to be addressed, for example, the sacrificial character of the Eucharist, the connection between the Eucharist and social justice, the growing ecumenical consensus about the Eucharist, the eschatological dimension of the Eucharist, and so on.

An ongoing effort to understand and to appreciate our immensely rich eucharistic tradition is necessary, and this ongoing commitment will enable us to understand our Christian identity as the Body of Christ as much as the Eucharist itself. As Augustine put it in the fourth century, 'Receive the body of Christ in holy Communion. Be what you receive.'[28]

8

THE EUCHARIST AND SOCIAL JUSTICE

Introduction

Many Catholics fail to see the relationship between the Eucharist and their lives. The Eucharist no longer speaks to their experience of life and appears to be something of a *superadditum* to what is really going on. It would be naive and lacking in historical awareness to believe that any one programme of action or theological/catechetical emphasis can solve all our difficulties in being Christians today. But is is the contention of this chapter that pointing up the links between the Eucharist and social justice may serve two functions in Christian communities: first, it may make the celebration more meaningful to those who experience a degree of alienation from the Eucharist; second, it may alert Christians to the social and political implications of their weekly assembly for worship, and so refuse to permit Christian faith to be made a marginal and privatised aspect of life.

Before proceeding it is important to give some indication of what is meant by 'social justice' in this context. While ethicists will give the expression their own nuances reflecting a variety of presuppositions about the nature of humankind, society and justice, the term is being used here in a broad sense. It has to do with the harmony and well-being of *all* in society, equality of basic opportunities and appropriate living conditions.

In his pamphlet *The Eucharist and Social Justice* David Morland writes:

> There is little sign... that the performance of the liturgy and the Eucharist in particular is an evident instrument of change in raising the consciousness of those who participate and in showing them how their worship is related to action for justice.'[1]

Reasons for this divorce between the Eucharist and social justice will reflect the circumstances of different persons, cultures and socio-political situations. But there are some theological factors which invite comment. First, there has been an excessive emphasis, especially since the Council of Trent, on the *ex opere operato* aspect of the sacramental event, with a consequent decrease of emphasis on the *ex opere operantis*. In other words, the exaggerated focus on the validity and the reality of the sacramental happening often led to a passivity on the part of the worshipping assembly. The reality of the sacrament was quite independent of their dispositions and contribution.

Another reason is that for many people the sacraments have become at times akin to magical rites. In paragraph 7 of *The Church in the Modern World*, there is praise for the critical ability to distinguish genuine religion from magic: '…people are taking a hard look at all magical world views, and prevailing superstitions and demanding a more personal and active commitment of faith…'.[2] The late Juan Luis Segundo comments on this text that implicit in the Council's words is the admission 'that in actual practice a magic-oriented tendency has taken over a large part of sacramental life'.[3] This magical tendency limits God's presence and activity to certain words or rites or places.

However, the fundamental and root cause for this separation of the Eucharist from social justice is a radical dualism which accepts a divorce between the sacred and the profane, between a person's everyday life and his/her religious life, between nature and grace. Since the rest of this chapter will be circling around this factor, no further comment is necessary here.

Inevitably, these factors taken together issue in a devotional piety with its privatised interests as a substitute for an ecclesial and responsible sacramental life. They have produced a mindset in which there is no evident connection between 'secular' action for justice and the 'sacred' celebration of the Eucharist, and sometimes a serious disjunction between being a Christian nationally and being a Christian in reality.

How does one counteract this privatised view of the Eucharist? How can one establish the centrality of social justice to the contemporary eucharistic experience and reflection of the community? It seems to me that the way forward theologically is to tease out the connection in relation to the tradition generally, and to the doctrines of eucharistic presence and sacrifice in particular.

The Christian tradition

Tradition is sometimes understood in a pejorative sense, referring not only to the past, but to the past seen as marginal, of little or no significance for the present. Behind this attitude lies an extrinsicist view that tradition exists outside of and alongside the person and the community. Clearly there is a degree of truth in this. The tradition as expressed in the Scriptures, the liturgy, the doctrines of the Church do have a certain existence over against the individual Christian. But the tradition is also 'inside' people, as it were. What we are now is shaped by the past. It seems more adequate, then, to think of tradition as constitutive of the person and the community, as the collective memory of the community, in which the communal wisdom and experience of the Church finds expression. The task of the theologian is not to impose the past as normative for the present, but rather to retrieve this collective wisdom and memory, to interpret the tradition in the light of its own historical assumptions and intentions, against the background of the need for a living understanding of the tradition today. It is in this sense that the link between the Eucharist/worship and social justice is thoroughly traditional.

Although the obvious bond between the Eucharist and social justice has been absent for the most part from the Council of Trent to Vatican II, for the reasons noted above, linking worship to social justice is nothing novel in the Jewish-Christian tradition. It finds its major expression in the Old Testament in the prophetic invective against an empty cult or a sacralism which guarantees salvation for the cheap price of a lip service orthodoxy. It is interesting to note Matthew Lamb's description of prophecy in his book, *Solidarity With Victims:* '…an agapic life or praxis whereby the cries of victims are articulated into a voice protesting the victimisation of humans by other humans.'[4]

The witness of the Old Testament

It seems to me that Lamb's contemporary description fits some of the prophetic critiques of the Old Testament, for example, Amos 5:21-25:

> The Lord says, 'I hate your religious festivals; I cannot stand them! When you bring me burnt offerings and grain offerings, I will not accept them; I will not accept the animals you have fattened to bring to me as offerings. Stop your noisy songs; I do not want to listen to your harps. Instead, let justice flow like a stream, and righteousness like a river that never goes dry.'

In this passage, the essential elements of Israel's worship – festivals, sacrifices, praise – are taken up one after another and rejected. Amos consistently uses righteousness and justice as terms for the qualities which ought to be present in the social order (6:12; 5:7, 15). 'Justice' refers to the judicial process through which right order is maintained in social relations, and in particular the protection of the weak and the poor through the help of the court. 'Righteousness' is the vital quality which characterises those who fulfil the responsibilities involved in their relationships. This condemnation of an empty cultic system is not peculiar to Amos alone, but appears to be something of a leitmotif running through the prophetic literature.

It is interesting to find this same critique in the Wisdom literature, in Sirach 34:18-22:

> If you offer as a sacrifice an animal that you have obtained dishonestly, it is defective and unacceptable. The Most High gets no pleasure from sacrifices made by ungodly people; no amount of sacrifices can make up for their sins. A man who steals an animal from the poor to offer as a sacrifice is like a man who kills a boy before his father's eyes. Food means life itself to poor people, and taking it away from them is murder. It is murder to deprive someone of his living or to cheat an employee of his wages.

The meaning of this passage is fairly self-evident but, according to his own testimony, it was this text which was instrumental in bringing about the conversion of Bartolomé de las Casas from being a colonial commander in Cuba to becoming a champion of the Indian cause. When preparing in 1514 to celebrate the Eucharist, de las Casas read this passage from Sirach, and, as a result of reflection on it, he freed his Indian slaves and for the rest of his life protested slavery in the Spanish dominions.[5]

The witness of the New Testament

Jesus inherited this prophetic critique of the cult, the clearest instance in the gospel record being Matthew 5:23-24, where he asserts the primacy of human relationships over worship:

> So if you are about to offer your gift at the altar and there you remember that your brother has something against you, leave your gift there in front of the altar, go at once and make peace with your brother, and then come back and offer your gift to God.

The foot-washing episode in John 13:1-20 may be considered in a similar way. It occurs within the narrative of the Last Supper and may be understood as the analogue of the institution narratives in the synoptic accounts. To say that it is analogous in function to the eucharistic narratives is to maintain that the action over the bread and wine and the foot-washing serve equally as prophetic gestures revealing the meaning of Jesus' death. Sandra Schneiders expresses this well:

> In the Johannine perspective what definitively distinguishes the community which Jesus calls into existence from the power structures so universal in human society is the love of friendship expressing itself in joyful mutual service for which rank is irrelevant.[6]

While is it must be said that there is no explicit link in our passages between the Eucharist and social justice, what is unmistakably clear is the emphasis on a new order of human relationships, the *sine qua non* for Eucharist and justice.

For a more explicit link we turn to St Paul in 1 Corinthians 11:17-34. For Paul the Christian community is an organic unity in which all the members are vitally related to each other through participation in a common life. This community demonstrates through its existence an understanding of humanity which is not dominated by the egocentricity that gives rise to possessiveness, divisiveness, strife. 'To enter this community is to abandon the individualism of self-affirmation.'[7] It is precisely this negative self-affirmation which Paul is denouncing in 1 Corinthians 11, most forcefully in verse 29:

> For if he does nor recognise the meaning of the Lord's body when he eats the bread and drinks from the cup, he brings judgment upon himself as he eats and drinks.

What does Paul mean by 'body' here? The words 'the Lord's' appear to be a scribal addition whose purpose is to underscore Paul's condemnation of the Corinthians failure to distinguish the Eucharist from ordinary food. But 'body' is capable of another interpretation, that it is an allusion to the community as the Lord's body. Already in a eucharistic context, in 1 Corinthians 10:17, Paul has stated that 'all of us, though many, are one body, for we all share the same loaf'. One may argue, therefore, that Paul's concern in 1 Corinthians 11 was not that the Corinthians were profaning a holy rite, but rather that they were fragmenting the community whose unity was signified in that rite. This nuance links the Eucharist intimately with human relationships, in our broad description, with 'social justice.'

Further examples from Christian authors

Later Christian writers, when championing the bond between the liturgy and social concern reinstated this prophetic insight of Amos, Isaiah, Jesus and Paul for their own times and circumstances. For example, Justin Martyr introduced his description of the community assembled for the Eucharist with these words: 'Those of us who have any resources come to the aid of all who are in need and we are always assisting on another.' And, near the end of his description: 'The wealthy who are willing, make contributions, each as he pleases, and the collection is deposited with the president, who aids widows and orphans, those who are in want because of sickness or some other reason, those in prison and visiting strangers – in short, he takes care of all in need.'

Something similar is instanced in the *Didascalia Apostolorum*:

> If a poor man or a poor woman comes, whether they are from your own parish or another, especially if they are advanced in years, and there should be no room for them, O bishop, then make a place for them with all your heart, even if you yourself have to sit on the ground. You must not make any distinction between persons, if you wish your ministry to be pleasing to God.[8]

One could continue to multiply such examples, and it is probably true to say that the link between the Eucharist and social justice was never entirely lost in the Church. Reformers like Francis of Assisi and Dominic, in founding religious communities in which the witness of vowed poverty was central, re-established the importance of this bond for the Church of their day. But beginning in the early Middle Ages, eucharistic theology in this particular respect fell on hard times. Most medieval theologians were exercised over the reality of the eucharistic presence of Christ and Christ's union with the soul of the believer, and seldom looked to the 'horizontal' aspect of eucharistic presence.

In contrast to the varied but complementary eucharistic theologies of the patristic period, there emerged a concentration on eucharistic presence and sacrifice, almost to the exclusion of all else. When we come, then, to the Council of Trent in the sixteenth century, it is these two aspects of eucharistic doctrine that the Council Fathers focus on in response to the Reformers. And the Catechism of the Council of Trent, which embodied its teachings for popular dissemination, perpetuated this exclusivist emphasis right into the twentieth century and up to the Second Vatican Council.[9]

In a number of significant places the Vatican Council, at least in principle, redressed the imbalance in eucharistic thinking and practice. I say 'in practice' for two reason. First, conciliar contributions to eucharistic theology took some considerable time to make an impact in this respect among sacramental theologians. Second, the Council treated of the Eucharist and social justice not so much directly in the *Constitution on he Sacred Liturgy*, as one might have expected, but rather indirectly in the *Constitution on The Church* and *The Church in the Modern World*. While on the surface this latter point may appear to be a strange way of proceeding, it becomes less strange when one recalls that the Eucharist is always an ecclesial action, the action of the entire community assembled to praise and give thanks. The question of the nature and purpose of this community is inescapably bound up with the understanding of the Eucharist. Out of the documents of the Council came new ecclesiological models, or better a retrieval of some traditional models which afford a more integrated understanding of the Church and the world, and so also of worship and the world. The theme of social justice receives particular attention in several places in the *Constitution on the Church*. For example, we read: ... the Church, in Christ, is in the nature of a sacrament – a sign and instrument, that is, of communion with God *and of unity among all men.*'[10] Since the Eucharist is seen as the summit and source of the Church's life it must be here above all else that the Church's commitment to social justice should be manifested and celebrated.

This same emphasis may be found in some ecumenical statements about the Eucharist, a good example being the *Les Dombes* Statement of 1972:

> Reconciled in the Eucharist, the members of the Body of Christ became the servants of reconciliation among men and witness to the joy of the resurrection... The celebration of the Eucharist, the breaking of bread that is necessary to life, is an incitement not to accept conditions in which men are deprived of bread, justice and peace.[11]

The doctrines of Eucharistic presence and sacrifice
No longer is it the case that the Catholic approach to the eucharistic presence of Christ identifies that presence exclusively with the eucharistic elements of bread and wine. As a result of both liturgical reform and ecumenical dialogue, as has been noted earlier in this volume, Christ is present in the proclamation of the Word, in the assembled community, in the person of the minister, as well as in the bread and wine. The Presence of Christ in the community as the Body of Christ is then as real as any of the other modes in which Christ is believed to be present, and this affords

yet another link between Eucharist and social justice. Again, this may be seen to be a traditional way of looking at the community and the Eucharist. In Sermon 272, cited at the end of the last chapter, St Augustine comments on how the priest presents the Eucharist with the phrase 'The Body of Christ', to which the Christian responds 'Amen'. He then continues; 'If you are the body and members of Christ, it is your mystery which is placed upon the Lord's table, it is your mystery which you receive…. Be what you see and receive what you are.' St John Chrysostom claimed that love of the poor was a liturgy whose altar was more venerable than the one on which the Eucharist was being celebrated, 'the latter being precious by reason of the body of Christ which is received [from it], the other because it *is* the body of Christ.[12] The presence of Christ in the community as the Body of Christ is an active presence, inviting and empowering the transformation of all through personal and social conversion. Conversion cannot be a vertical movement to the divine without the horizontal relationship to man and the world. History is one history, not to be dichotomised into sacred and secular histories running alongside each other. And so, working for justice in the world, for the liberation of humankind, is necessary to the community as the embodiment of Christ's presence celebrating the Eucharist. What makes this community different from other groups working for justice in the world is that the Church is the embodied sign of Christ's transforming presence.

Since at least the time of the Reformation, sacrifice has been a divisive aspect of eucharistic doctrine. There are powerful signs that this is changing. The Windsor Agreed Statement of the Anglican-Roman Catholic International Commission, from a bilateral perspective, and the Lima Statement, from a multilateral perspective, for example, both witness to the one, unique, all-sufficient sacrifice of Christ and to the re-presentation of this in the eucharistic memorial, the *anamnesis* of Calvary.

This *anamnesis* approach to eucharistic sacrifice may gain

strength from the work of Johann Baptist Metz on memory, and in a way which will integrate this aspect of eucharistic doctrine with social justice. Metz, in explicating the Eucharist as *memoria passionis,* the memory of the passion and death of Christ, establishes that the suffering of Christ was due to the religious, social and political powers of his day. When that suffering is remembered and recalled in the Eucharist, the contemporary power structures that allow continued suffering, oppression, injustice are called into question:

> In the light of the Christian memory of suffering, it is clear that social power and political domination are not simply to be taken for granted but that they continually have to justify themselves in view of actual suffering.... The social and political power of the rich and the rulers must be open to the question of the extent to which it causes suffering ... The Christian memory of suffering can become, alongside many other often subversive, innovative factors in our society, the ferment for that new political life we are seeking on behalf of our future.[13]

The dynamic sense of memorial in the light of Metz's comments, allied to an integral awareness of being the body of Christ becomes, or at least has the capacity to become, a mighty catalyst in our ecclesial commitment to justice.

Conclusion

I hope it is clear from these remarks that my intention has not been so to emphasise the bond between the Eucharist and social justice as to marginalise other important aspects of eucharistic doctrine. Nor has it been my intention to reduce the liturgy to a platform for party politics. My aim has been to show that commitment to social justice is not an optional extra for a Christian, but is knit into the very fabric of eucharistic worship, and that reflection on this is an intrinsic component of eucharistic theology; and that the attempt to tease out the relationship between the Eucharist and social justice may be of direct pastoral relevance today. Worship without social commitment becomes reduced to mere sentimentality and commitment without worship and prayer often becomes grim and barbaric. What is required today is unity between worship-prayer and commitment to work for a more just social order.

9

THE ECUMENICAL EUCHARISTIC THEOLOGY OF JOHN MACQUARRIE

Introduction

As the Second Vatican Council drew to a close in 1965, John Macquarrie made his way from the Church of Scotland to the Anglican Communion, being ordained priest by Bishop Donegan of New York. Macquarrie, Lady Margaret Professor of Divinity Emeritus in the University of Oxford, is probably best known for his contributions to philosophical theology and, in fact, the *Macquarrie-Festschrift* is almost entirely devoted to topics in that discipline. The one exception is the fine essay by Enda McDonagh entitled 'Sacraments and Society'. Curiously, however, although McDonagh makes reference 'to the seriousness with which John Macquarrie has taken sacraments and sacramentality in his theological work and personal life', he does not refer once to anything Macquarrie has written on sacramental theology.[1] The reason may be that Macquarrie never produced a book exclusively given over to sacramental theology until his recent *A Guide to the Sacraments* (1997).[2] Even before this, however, there are abundant references to the sacraments and especially the Eucharist throughout the entire Macquarrie *corpus*. This essay is an exploration of his eucharistic theology.

There is a purple passage in *Paths in Spirituality* which reveals the comprehensiveness, the depth and the richness of Macquarrie's eucharistic theology, and which deserves to be quoted in full:

> The Eucharist sums up in itself Christian worship, experience and theology in an amazing richness. It seems to include everything. It combines Word and Sacrament;

its appeal is to spirit and to sense; it brings together the sacrifice of Calvary and the presence of the risen Christ; it is communion with God and communion with man; it covers the whole gamut of religious moods and emotions. Again, it teaches the doctrine of creation, as the bread, the wine and ourselves are brought to God; the doctrine of atonement, for these gifts have to be broken in order that they may be perfected; the doctrine of salvation, for the Eucharist has to do with incorporation into Christ and the sanctification of human life; above all, the doctrine of incarnation, for it is no distant God whom Christians worship but one who has made himself accessible in the world. The Eucharist also gathers up in itself the meaning of the Church; its whole action implies and sets forth our mutual interdependence in the body of Christ; it unites us with the Church of the past and even, through its paschal overtones, with the first people of God, as an anticipation of the heavenly banquet. Comprehensive though this description is, it is likely that I have missed something out, for the Eucharist seems to be inexhaustible.[3]

If ever a statement were needed demonstrating clearly the integration of eucharistic belief and theology with the entire fabric of Christian doctrine, this is it. The Eucharist is related to all of life and theology. At the same time, he notes that in the history of the Christian tradition there have been different emphases on various aspects of the Eucharist. This is almost impossible to avoid, but 'it is only wrong when one aspect is stressed to the exclusion of others, and this has sometimes happened'.[4] To avoid such forms of exclusion Macquarrie deliberately sets out to articulate eucharistic theology in a way that would be acceptable to 'most of the major communions of the Christian Church'.[5]

This interpretation of the sacrament, consonant with his

systematic theology as a whole, is in existential-ontological terms. This way of proceeding is typically expressive of the *via media anglicana*.[6] As existential, the eucharistic reality cannot be understood in purely objective terms, and cannot be an event that takes place *extra nos*. As ontological, the eucharistic reality cannot be founded on any merely subjective appreciation of the sacrament. 'The Eucharist is decidedly not a mere memorial or a way of helping us to remember what Christ did a long time ago. It is a genuine re-presenting of Christ's work. In this sacrament, as in the others, the initiative is with God; it is he who acts in the sacrament and makes himself present.'[7] From a traditional Catholic point of view, Macquarrie's perspective tensively holds together the *ex opere operato* and the *ex opere operantis* dimensions of the sacrament.

The Eucharistic sacrifice

While he obviously distances himself from viewing the Eucharist as a *memoria Christi* in a subjectivist sense, curiously there seems to be a degree of ambivalence in Macquarrie's handling of the notion of memorial/*anamnesis*. On the other hand, he seems to fault ARCIC I's *Windsor Statement on the Eucharist*: '…for some reason ARCIC was very biblicist in its treatment of the Eucharist. Thus the difficult notions of eucharistic sacrifice and eucharistic presence were made to rest very largely on a highly dynamic exegesis of the Greek word *anamnesis*, "memorial". The exegesis may be correct, but there are scholars who contest it, and *by itself* it provides an insecure base for what ARCIC wanted to say.'[8] This is an unnecessarily harsh interpretation of ARCIC's use of *anamnesis*, which is not faulted by the formal 'Responses' of the Church of England[9] or of the Catholic Bishops of England and Wales.[10] In fact, the *only* dissenting scholar that Macquarrie presents is the Evangelical Anglican, Philip E. Hughes.[11]

On the other hand, in his more recent *Jesus Christ in Modern Thought* he develops a much more favourable reaction to *anamnesis,* this time relying especially upon the contribution of Joachim Jeremias: 'A further point made by Jeremias and again commonly accepted by liturgical scholars, is that *anamnesis* does not mean just a remembering of the past: "God's remembrance is never a simple remembering of something, but always an effecting and creating event."[12] Thus, Macquarrie ends up with an interpretation of *anamnesis* more consistent with his existential-ontological methodology. The Christian assembly remembers, that is represents, the unique saving action of Christ in the Eucharist, but the foundation of the assembly's remembering is the efficacious, creative 'remembrance' of God. Macquarrie's understanding here is entirely consonant with the expression and meaning of ARCIC I's *Windsor Statement on the Eucharist,* paragraph 5:

> …The notion of *memorial* as understood in the passover celebration at the time of Christ – i.e. the making effective in the present of an event in the past – has opened the way to a clear understanding of the relationship between Christ's sacrifice and the Eucharist. The eucharistic memorial is no mere calling to mind of a past event or its significance, but the Church's effectual proclamation of God's mighty acts.

Macquarrie's treatment of eucharistic sacrifice is quite brief in contrast to his consideration of the 'real presence' of Christ. With respect to eucharistic sacrifice, Macquarrie sees its origins immediately in the events of the Last Supper and the death of Christ. Ultimately, however, sacrifice is self-giving, and self-giving is characteristic of the very life and existence of God; 'Self-giving was characteristic of God himself in his act of creation. In the history of creation, that self-giving came to its climactic moment in the incarnation and in Christ's giving himself up to death.'[13] The self-giving does not end there, but reaches into the liturgical assembly, the people of God. 'The people of God can realise itself as that people only to the extent that sacrifice and self-giving has been taken into the very essence of its life.'[14] This sacrificial self-giving is simultaneously the ultimate realisation of human potential, not in a pelagian sense, but in the sense of surrender to and conformity with the very being of God. The sacrifice of the Eucharist is the ritual focus that unites protology and eschatology, christology and ecclesiology, and each one of these doctrines is but comment on the Self-Giving that the mystery of the Trinity is.

Within the eucharistic rite itself two moments especially touch on the ideal of sacrifice: the *offertory* (the offering of the bread and wine before the consecration), and the *oblation* (the offering of these elements after the consecration).[15] In the offertory the bread and wine stand for the people of the assembly themselves as they co-operate with and submit to God in response to the initiative of God's self-giving, proclaimed in the liturgy of the Word. In contrast, the oblation 'is done by the priest alone, for in this he is acting in Christ's place, and this means that it is Christ who makes the oblation'.[16] This affirmation that the priest is acting 'in Christ's place' takes Macquarrie into a consideration of ordained ministry through the notion of 'character', but in a particularly nuanced fashion.

He eschews a purely functionalist approach to ordination. He insists that the ordained ministers are not simply persons authorised to perform specific functions within the Church, that there is an ontological dimension to ordination, traditionally designated by the word 'character'.[17] 'Character' is best understood as a formation and pattern of personal being. 'It is through the doing of acts that character is formed, then character in turns informs the acts.'[18] The character of baptism and confirmation is not instantly injected into the person, as if in some magical way. Christians grow into the character of their baptism/confirmation, initiated on the day of ritual celebration.

The character of ordination is to be understood similarly. 'Priesthood is a lifetime commitment and a lifelong vocation, and indeed takes the best part of a lifetime for the full flowering of priestly character.'[19] What has been referred to traditionally as the 'indelibility' of the character expresses primarily God's faithfulness to his enabling grace and consequently, the irreversibility of the process initiated by ordination. The fact that the process may be arrested or not exercised by some of the ordained cannot detract from the self-giving faithfulness of God in the act of ordination.[20] While, however, the ministry of the ordained remains distinctive within the Church, it is integrated into and is continuous with the general ministry of the Church established through baptism/confirmation.

Nowhere in Macquarrie's *corpus* can one find any very detailed account of Anglican debate about eucharistic sacrifice such as that of the late Richard P. C. Hanson and Rowan Williams.[21] The only reasonable conclusion is that he viewed the matter sufficiently explored and resolved within the frame of his own theology, and, therefore, that it required no further comment. Unlike Hanson and Williams, Macquarrie seems to have little time for the nuances and subtleties of historical theology on this particular issue. His methodological bias is avowedly philosophical, but careful, even if brief, attention to the historical evolution of the doctrine of eucharistic sacrifice would both enhance and strengthen his solid judgement.

Eucharistic presence

God is acknowledged in the Christian tradition to be universally present to his creation, and Jesus Christ as the divine Logos is, therefore, also universally present.[22] How is this acknowledgement of the universal presence of the Triune God to be reconciled with the idea of a particular presence, for example, in the Incarnation, in the Church and the sacraments? Macquarrie's response is to affirm that it would be virtually impossible to recognise the universal presence if there were no particular presences:

> ...it is very important not to let particular presences be simply swallowed up on a universal presence. I doubt very much whether such a universal presence could ever be detected or recognised unless we were pointed to it by particular presences, moments of intensity, of meeting or encounter. It is part of our human nature to seek those particular occasions'.[23]

Thus, in the Old Testament, the ark of the covenant, the tabernacle, the temple, the *shekinah*, are to be understood as centres which focused with intensity God's universal presence for the ancient Hebrews.

In respect of the Eucharist, just as the entire celebration falls into two distinct parts, the liturgy of the Word and the liturgy of the Eucharist, so the recognition of Christ's presence takes this twofold shape. In the liturgy of the Word, the climax of this recognition is the proclamation of the Gospel; in the liturgy of the Eucharist the climax occurs in the consecrated elements.[24] Secondly, Macquarrie sees the congregation's response to the presence in the word coming in the communal affirmation of the creed, and the presence in the consecrated elements in the reception of holy communion. Finally, two ritual gestures express in a parallel fashion this dual mode of Christ's presence: the elevation of the book of the Gospels and the elevation of the eucharistic gifts.[25]

In speaking of the 'Body of Christ', care must be taken to note the threefold significance of the term. Literally, the term applies to the 'actual personal being-in-the world' of the historical Jesus of Nazareth. The Body of Christ is also the sacramental host, representing Christ and received in communion. The Body of Christ is at the same time the worshipping assembly, incorporated into Christ through baptism and confirmation, 'and now being steadily conformed to him through participation in the Eucharist'.[26]

After commenting on the eucharistic presence of Christ as temporal and as spiritual, Macquarrie opts for the category of 'personal presence' as the most appropriate. Personal presence is not, however, to be construed as synonymous with purely 'spiritual' presence, because 'a person is embodied and includes a physical presence'.[27] His notion of personal presence transcends the typical representation of the subject-object pattern. Personal presence is objective/ontological because it entirely depends on the initiative of Holy Being epiphanied in particular beings, the eucharistic elements of bread and wine. At the same time, the presence is just as much subjective/existential, insofar as this particular manifestation of Holy Being occurs only in the context of the Body of Christ, understood in the polyvalent sense noted above. Here again is seen the continuous application of Macquarrie's existential-ontological theism.

As with all personal presence, the personal presence of Christ in the Eucharist is multidimensional. Christ is present in his body, the community, in the presiding minister, in the word, as well as in the consecrated elements. '…Christ is present *par excellence* in the consecrated bread and wine'.[28] Macquarrie warns about trying to fix a 'moment of consecration' too precisely, insisting that 'the whole prayer of consecration consecrates'.[29]

This multidimensional, personal presence of Christ in the Eucharist has been expounded in various theories employing philosophical categories such as 'substance', 'significance', 'value'. The central issue is belief in a real abiding eucharistic presence, but a degree of theological pluralism in articulating this belief is both permissible and desirable.[30]

Macquarrie gives attention to substance/transubstantiation and significance/transsignification, but not to value/transvaluation, though this was the favoured mode of expression for the eucharistic presence of Archbishop William Temple in his illumination *Christus Veritas.*[31] He notes that the doctrine of transubstantiation has been dominant in the Western Church for a long time.[32] He considers it historically important as 'the official eucharistic theology of the Roman Catholic Church... even if it is no longer held to be explanatory', though he does not subscribe to it himself.[33] Distancing himself from Protestant polemicists, Macquarrie affirms that transubstantiation has absolutely nothing to do with a magical approach to the Eucharist, and, in fact, is best regarded as one of the most solid defenses against such a position.[34] According to this theory of eucharistic presence, there is no sensible difference whatsoever in the eucharistic elements before and after consecration. 'Physics and chemistry have got nothing to do with what happens in consecration; or, to put it in different language, one could never get any empirical verification of the presence of Christ in the consecrated elements.'[35] The presence of Christ is perceptible only to the eyes of faith, to 'a seeing in depth', and Macquarrie is fond of citing the words of St Thomas Aquinas: '*Praestet fides supplementum sensuum defectui*.'[36]

While St Thomas may be the architect of transubstantiation, it does not originate with him. While the term had been used occasionally, it was first officially sanctioned by the Fourth Lateran Council in 1215.[37] This Council asserted the '*corpus et sanguis (Jesu Christi) in sacramento altaris sub speciebus panis et vini veraciter continentur, transsubstantiationis pani corpus et vino in sanguinem potestate divina.*'[38] The statement, in Macquarrie's judgement, is careful, especially the emphasis that the transformation comes about *potestate divina* It was St Thomas, however, who was to flesh out the details of the meaning of 'substance'. For St Thomas 'substance' is a metaphysical term, not to be identified with physical matter. For St Thomas the accidents of bread and wine remain unchanged. 'Substance' language, therefore, affirms a doctrine of eucharistic presence that is realistic without being materialistic or physicalist. When, however, the austere language of the Lateran Council and of St Thomas is set alongside the statement about transubstantiation from the Council of Constance in 1417, there have occurred some significant changes. In the decrees of Constance we read: '*Item, utrum credat, quod post consecrationem sacerdotis in sacramento altaris sub velamento panis et vini non sit panis materialis et vinum materiale, sed idem per omni Christus.*'[39] As Macquarrie interprets this language, there is reference here not to a metaphysical change of substance, but rather substance has been identified with physical matter. Material bread and wine have been 'replaced' by the body and blood of Christ. Furthermore, the transformation is not effected *potestate divina*, but *post consecrationem sacerdotis*.[40] The originally austere doctrine of transubstantiation had degenerated into 'the semi-magical teaching which the Reformers knew as transubstantiation and which they rejected, as in article 28 of the *Book of Common Prayer.*'[41] The real defect of the eucharistic language of Constance is the denial of the sacramental/incarnational principle whereby material realities become ontologically the presence of the divine, but without ceasing to be material realities. The Reformers latched onto the defective or corrupt form of transubstantiation but failed to advert to the earlier, most positive forms of the doctrine.

The Council of Trent is more in harmony with the earlier form of transubstantiation than the Council of Constance. While Trent affirms a real or substantial change in the eucharistic elements, this is never teased out too precisely. The 'how' of Christ's presence in the Eucharist is not explained and 'it is simply claimed that the word is one that may be suitably (*convenienter, proprie, aptissime*) used, and has been so used by the Church'.[42] Macquarrie rightly sees this approach to transubstantiation reflected in the ARCIC Agreed Statement on the Eucharist.

While genuinely appreciative of transubstantiation, Macquarrie is critical of it. He takes notice of Schillebeeckx's interpretation of Trent: 'At Trent the word "transubstantiation" explained nothing, but simply stood for the Catholic as against the Protestant understanding of the Eucharist.'[43] This is, firstly, an oversimplification because there is no one 'Protestant' way of understanding the Eucharist.[44] Secondly, however, if the word simply affirms a 'real presence' of Christ in the Eucharist without any explanatory theory (the 'how' of that presence), then the term is quite misleading. It is misleading because it suggests the entire Aristotelian-Thomist philosophical apparatus of hylomorphism, and 'this philosophical apparatus is not one that readily commends itself today'.[45] His own existential-ontological view understands the world not as 'an aggregate of substances, but as a structure of meaning'.[46] Finally, Macquarrie considers the language of hylomorphism inappropriate because it is impersonal language, whereas the language of eucharistic presence is best understood in personal terms.[47]

Another theological theory, which is just as capable as transubstantiation of sustaining a deep and rich eucharistic faith and practice, is transsignification. The philosophical backdrop of this theory is the phenomenological and existentialist categories of Husserl, Merleau-Ponty and Heidegger. In this philosophical tradition reality is not constituted by 'thinghood' or, we might say, 'substance', but by 'a personally structured totality of meanings'.[48] This does not render reality the construal of the subject, finally expressed as some form of idealism. Rather, the linguistic and significant community, of which the individual is part and to which he contributes, determines meaning and reality. This is central to Macquarrie's existential-ontological theism, and seems to bear a strong family resemblance to the post-liberal theology of George A. Lindbeck. The linguistic-cultural perspective of the individual is established through and by a linguistic-cultural community, in this instance the Church.[49] Macquarrie writes:

> The effect of the language [of the eucharistic action] is to shift the elements out of the one region of signification into another – from the everyday world into the setting of the eucharistic community. This is not a subjective view of presence, if one accepts that significance enters into the ontological constitution of a thing; but neither is it an objective view, as if the body and blood of Christ existed outside the context of the eucharistic community, which is also this body.[50]

Macquarrie does not maintain that his version of existential-ontological theism applied to eucharistic presence is identical with transsignification as understood by Catholic scholars, but only that it is 'close to' it, and is preferable to transubstantiation.[51] For Macquarrie, '…no theory of eucharistic presence can ever be more than an approximation',[52] which could well stand as a twentieth century paraphrase of what the Anglican divine Lancelot Andrews said to Cardinal Robert Bellarmine: '…we believe no less than you that the presence is real, but concerning the mode of that presence we define nothing rashly'.[53]

Eucharistic reservation

'What happens to the consecrated elements at the end of the Eucharist? What people do with them is often a good guide to what theology of presence they hold…'.[54] If this axiom is applied to John Macquarrie, then what emerges is a very high theology of presence indeed. He maintains that the primary aim of reservation is the communion of the sick and of those unable to attend the Eucharist, and he is aware that this practice may be traced back to Justin Martyr and the *Apostolic Tradition*.[55] Yet, reservation for the sick cannot be isolated and includes latent possibilities for devotion:

> For the sacrament cannot be retained or reserved in a merely casual way, as if one could be resolved to take a

precious gift to the sick and yet be also resolved to treat that gift lightly.[56]

A proper reverence for the reserved Eucharist may issue in personal prayer and devotion, the kind of devotion which seeks to extend the Eucharist to all of life that it may be conformed to its living Lord.[57] The key eucharistic devotional practice is Benediction, of which Macquarrie is a staunch advocate. 'Psychologically speaking, we need some concrete visible manifestation toward which to direct our devotion; while theologically speaking, this is already provided for us by our Lord's gracious manifestation of his presence in the Blessed Sacrament.'[58]

Conclusion

Macquarrie writes of theologians: 'Theologians can only too easily begin to think of themselves as the *teleoi,* those who attained to a *gnosis* that is beyond the reach of the ordinary faithful.'[59] This is not a temptation to which John Macquarrie himself has succumbed. John S. Bowden, Macquarrie's publisher and editor at the Student Christian Movement Press in London, has this to say about him: 'He has proved a successful mediator between the academic world and the parishes in producing a believing form of academic theology.'[60] It is fashionable today to speak of theology having three publics – the Church, the academy, and society – but perhaps less fashionable to see theology in the academy serving the faith of the Church. If Bowden is correct, then John Macquarrie has consistently tried to serve the faith of the Church, and the Church understood in the widest sense, in its catholicity, and not only his own Anglican Communion. His eucharistic theology services well his own ecclesial tradition, but it speaks powerfully to Rome and Geneva as well as to Canterbury. He knows, respects, and loves the eucharistic tradition, and yet in his retrieval of it he is critical. The cause of ecumenism is advanced not only through official, ecclesial dialogues, but also through the creative, careful mediation of theology to worshipping communities by theologians like John Macquarrie.

10

LITURGY AND THE PARISH

What makes for good liturgy in the parish? Not an easy question to tackle, not least because one's answer is necessarily self-revealing. I am convinced that while there is no quick-fix formula for good liturgy, there are some basic considerations that can improve our liturgical celebrations. But, before moving to these, let's begin with some words about the 'new' liturgy that emerged after the Second Vatican Council.

> Wherever one goes these days… Catholics seem to be at loggerheads about liturgy. Some dream with nostalgia of the old rite (Pius V, 1570), deploring the all but total disappearance of the Latin language and Gregorian chant; others are irked (now that they have been made conscious of liturgy and the possibility of changing it) either by the manner in which the new rite is performed in their locality or by the failure to reform it much more radically. Some feel they have been arbitrarily bereft of a rite that expressed their experience of God in faith as adequately as anything ever could; while others feel that they have had imposed upon them a compromise rite, bookish and wordy, that doesn't (now they have come to reflect on such matters) embody or direct the very secular and reticent groping for God in the ambiguity of faith which seems their personal experience… But some of the prevailing malaise is surely unnecessary and it seems worth while trying to dissipate it.[1]

These words of Fr Fergus Kerr OP, penned twenty-six years ago, could be said to describe our own times. They have a contemporary ring to them. As the process of liturgical revision continues, not only are Fr Kerr's words descriptive of the people in the pews, but increasingly also of the community of liturgical scholars.

Recently, Mgr Francis Mannion, commenting on the diversity of views among liturgical reformers, has come up with five positions describing the contemporary scene in the United States, but *mutatis mutandis*, his comments hold good for the United Kingdom and Ireland. First are those who advance the official liturgical reform consequent upon the Vatican Council. The other positions stand in relation to this one. Second, and at the traditionalist end of the spectrum, are those who would restore the pre-conciliar liturgy. While there are differences among this group, they all seem to share the basic conviction that the authentic liturgy of the Church has been compromised by the Council. Third are the reformers of the reform, who contend that the reform was poorly conceived and poorly implemented. A fresh reform must be initiated. Fourth, are the inculturators of the reform, who, now that all the rites have been thoroughly revised, desire the adaptation of the rites to various cultures. Finally, come those who advocate a 'recatholicising' of the reform. The recatholicising agenda is committed to the following objective: to a 'vital recreation of the ethos that has traditionally imbued Catholic liturgy at its best – an ethos of beauty, majesty, spiritual profundity and solemnity.'[2] What is necessary is not further liturgical change, but a deeper and richer appropriation of our present liturgy. This particular essay on liturgy in the parish is closely associated with Mannion's recatholicising of the reform.

The *Constitution on the Liturgy* reads (§14):

> Mother Church earnestly desires that all the faithful should be led to that full, conscious and active participation in liturgical celebrations which is demanded by the very nature of the liturgy, and to which the Christian people... have a right and obligation by reason of their baptism.[3]

The Constitution continues by insisting that this full and active participation 'is the aim to be considered before all else', and that pastors of souls 'should energetically set about achieving it through the requisite pedagogy'.[4] The following reflections address the question, 'How are the faithful to be led to that full, conscious and active participation?', or 'What is the requisite pedagogy for achieving such participation?' The answer to the question, the appropriate pedagogy, may be unfolded in five steps.

Step 1: Liturgical literacy is the key without which the sacred mysteries will remain a treasure in a locked room.

In order fully to appreciate any expression of human culture, it is necessary to be inducted into an understanding of what is going on. What is not understood is ignored.

Leaving aside the particularities of any given example, one hears the constant complaint from teachers at all levels of a pervasive, cultural illiteracy. The American writer and educationalist, E. D. Hirsch, describes the phenomenon of cultural illiteracy in these words: 'Believing that a few direct experiences would suffice to develop the skills that children require, Dewey assumed that early education need not be tied to specific content. He mistook a half-truth for the whole. He placed too much faith in children's ability to learn general skills from a few typical experiences, and too hastily rejected "the piling up of information". Only by piling up specific community-based information can children learn to participate in complex cooperative activities with other members of their community.'[5] Hirsch insists that children learn to become skilled and responsible members of society by learning the 'stuff' of that society. Absorbing the stories and lore of a tradition, appropriating (initially through constant performance, and later through informed intellectual analysis) the ritual gestures of a tradition, enables children to take their mature place in society.

Induction into the liturgy takes place in the same way. First, we need to have a basic level of ritual competence through imitative, affiliative repetition. Then, as we grow psychologically and intellectually, we need a proportionate explanation of what these rites mean. That is liturgical literacy. We move from pre-reflective, liturgical performance to reflective and informed liturgical participation. Full, active and conscious participation in anything comes about through nurture, education, study. There is nothing magical about liturgical participation. It comes about through gradual and informed exposure to its meaning through various forms of teaching. It is true that the liturgy should not be didactic in any narrow construal of that word. If liturgy is praising the Father, in the Son, through the Spirit, then it is not a classroom lesson. However, without classroom lessons what people are doing in the praise and worship of God will be so much the less.

There is good precedent for this approach to liturgical literacy in the patristic era, especially the period of the great mystagogical catechises of the fifth-century fathers. When the catechumens of the great urban centres of Jerusalem and Milan, for example, had been initiated into the Church through baptism-anointing-eucharist by Cyril and Ambrose, *then* they were formally inducted into the full meaning of the liturgical mysteries. Liturgical literacy, carefully prepared for through scriptural and moral literacy, was the preoccupation of the bishop-catechist during the period of mystagogia.

No one would deny that children need to be prepared for Confirmation, First Communion, first Penance. Liturgical fluency does end with basic literacy. If fluency is to emerge for the adult active participants in our congregations, then they must learn more about the liturgy, and provision must be made for that learning through programmes of preparation for infant baptism, marriage preparation programmes that unpack practice from the liturgical rite, and so forth. It is not so much a matter of creating *de novo* programmes of liturgical theology, as much as it is tapping into those key ritual moments that occur in the life cycle and enhancing their appreciation through pastorally sensitive, structured learning.

Step 2: While it is axiomatic that the liturgy is 'the source and summit' of the activity of the Church, much else needs to happen in the parish.

The centre of the liturgy is, of course, the Eucharist, and for most people this celebration   occurs   on   the   Lord's   Day.   Sunday Eucharist is *the* occasion when we are called to experience the liturgy as the source and summit of our lives. However, between one Sunday and the next, the faithful remain a baptised and eucharistic people, and are sent out into the world as such a eucharistic people. As Paul McPartlan has put it recently, 'The Eucharist not only *gathers* the Church, it then *sends us out*, renewed, to gather the world.'[6] Gathered, re-affirmed and restored as Body of Christ in and through the Eucharist, we are called to act as that Body in our world. The world is gathered through the mediated immediacy of our gathering. In eucharistic mission, we are to have the mind, and so also the actions of Christ, as those are summarised by him in the synagogue at Nazareth: to bring good news to the poor and afflicted, to proclaim liberty to captives, to give sight to the blind, to lift the burdens of oppression (Luke 4:18ff.). Caring for others, healing the sick, *bringing* good news to the poor by *being* good news to and among the poor, are the means by which we, under grace, gather the world.

· In practical terms, this gathering of the world will involve parochial plans to enable justice to flourish in our communities. Programmes of voluntary action for justice and charitable outreach are demanded by the Eucharist as its moral face in the world.[7] Our eucharistic attitudes need to go beyond the somewhat safe pale of work for justice to embrace everything. We leave Mass to embody in our entire lives – in our families, homes, with our spouses and children, in places of employment and work, in recreation and fun, on the highway – the One whose Body we have eaten. In a word, the celebration of Eucharist cannot be the source and summit of our lives if our lives themselves are not striving to be eucharistic in all our contextual circumstances and situations.

Step 3: Take care of the details of the liturgy because God is to be encountered in the details.

The *Constitution on the Liturgy* (§34) notes that 'The rites should be distinguished by a noble simplicity…'. The real challenge is to know in what simplicity consists. 'Simplicity' is not a value-free term, but comes laden with a host of presuppositions. At the risk of oversimplification *(sic!)*, it might be said that in the broad Christian tradition there are two fundamental models of simplicity, expressing the two fundamental shapes of the Christian imagination, the analogical and the dialectical.[8] From the standpoint of the dialectical imagination, giving emphasis to God's utter transcendence and reflecting principally the Reformation tradition, simplicity may consist in lack of ornamentation and ritual richness, focusing as it does on the presence of the Word of God. On the other hand, the Catholic analogical imagination will enjoy a more expansive appreciation of 'simplicity', manifesting and celebrating God's presence as radically immanent. Simplicity in this context will not consist in stripping down the liturgy to its most basic, nude, component parts, but rather in the perfect harmonising of the complex forms and parts of the entire liturgical celebration.

In practice, this will mean taking care of the details of the liturgy, as so many *loci* in which the Mystery of God is to be encountered and engaged. Careful attention to the details of the celebration is the pre-requisite for enabling mystagogy. Indeed, one might say anything other than due care of *all* the details of liturgical celebration, of the twists and turns of the rites, smacks of liturgical docetism, that is to say, the Spirit-led encounter with Christ, and the location in him before the Father is impossible without the 'flesh and bones' of liturgical detail.

This is the particular care and concern of the various liturgical ministers: checking that all the liturgical vessels are in place, that books are properly marked; that all liturgical ministers know exactly what to do and how to do it, so that no one gets in the way of the mystagogy. To enable that kind of competent, ministerial choreography means that people need to be taken through their paces by someone who is competent to do so. And again and again, until they have got it right! It is impossible to enter into the prayer of the Easter Vigil, for example, unless everything is in place and has been attended to ahead of time, especially if one is about to be baptised or received into the Church. Mistakes will always happen in liturgical celebrations and are virtually unavoidable, but when they occur due to habitual carelessness, something is fundamentally wrong. While it may be acknowledged that an obsession with the details so as to produce the harmony that eases the encounter with God may lead to liturgical monophysitism, this seems not to be in the forefront of sins against the liturgy in our time.

Step 4: Liturgy must be predictable for the people to have ownership and to be actively participant.

Liturgy is predictable if it occurs in the same basic pattern with regularity. The comfort level for ritual increases, and so, therefore, the capacity for graceful encounter with God when people know what to expect, what to say, what to do.

This is the principle to which David Martin alludes when he affirms that 'Norms, standards, formulae, routines… exist to stabilise the molten wax of vision and pass on the imprint.'[9] Our attitudes, our prayerful and normally ill-thought-out changes in the drama of the liturgy are disturbances that affect not only the congregation's comfort and identity. They do more. The abandonment of liturgical stability and predictability also affect our sense of Transcendent Mystery. It is as if the flow of the 'text' that is the liturgy, interpolated with spontaneous gloss even of a broadly theological nature, is no longer able to induct us into the sense of God. All the constructs of the liturgy intend such a sense, but if they are to work, to be effective, predictability and stability of performance are required. Spontaneity and conviviality certainly have their place at times in the liturgy, but when they intrude upon the predictability of the liturgy they become singularly dysfunctional. At Mass some weeks ago, a visiting priest at the Communion Rite went on for some time at 'This is the Lamb of God, who takes away the sin of the world...'. I, and no doubt the other members of the congregation, wanted to say the prayer, 'Lord, I am not worthy...', but, since no one knew *when* to say the prayer because of the priest's extemporising, no one actually said it! The prayer is important when going to Holy Communion, but on that occasion was taken from the people.

Step 5: Priest are stewards of the mysteries, not liturgical entrepreneurs.

What is required of the priest, and what the people have a right to expect, is that he celebrates the liturgy according to the mind of the Church, as that finds expression in the liturgical books. That is proper 'presidential style'. The celebrant does not have to make up the liturgy as he goes along, does not have to devise new techniques to engage the people, because the liturgical mysteries are not his. They belong to *all* the people of the Church. The ministers are stewards of the mysteries. This contrasts sharply with what has been described as 'the game-show' approach to eucharistic presidency which seems to focus unduly on the priestly role. The people (even when entertained) are passive spectators at a priestly event. By the same token, when priests take liberties in changing official texts or improvising on ritual elements, the liturgical rite is destabilised and the people are disenfranchised and marginalised.'[10] Good liturgy and good liturgical presidency aim at letting the rites shape self-understanding and ecclesial understanding, so that that understanding may be passed on to the next generation, and the next after them. That is what stewardship is about. It does not imply a spurious kind of freedom to do whatever one wants with what has been entrusted to one.

Before beginning work on this article, I asked my sixteen-year-old son the question, 'Why is good liturgy important for a parish?' This was his response: 'So that the parish has a closer sense of togetherness, a stronger grasp of its faith, so that the parish understands the real reason for being there – to worship God.' My response to the question in this article is really a series of glosses on his. The unity of the parish, a growing grasp of the faith, the worship of God comes about when the liturgy is celebrated well, and the five steps outlined above seem to me to secure good celebration.

NOTES

Chapter 1: Cyprian of Carthage and Ephrem of Nisibis – Two Patristic Approaches to the Eucharist

1. Thomas C. Oden, *Requiem* (Nashville: Abingdon Press, 1995). A very fair-minded but critical response to Oden may be found in Donald E. Meisser, *Calling Church and Seminary Into the 21st Century* (Nashville: Abingdon Press, 1995). Concerns similar to those of Oden are expressed in David H. Kelsey, *To Understand God Truly: What's Theological About a Theological School?* (Louisville: Westminster/John Knox Press, 1992), and *Between Athens and Berlin: The Theological Education Debate* (Grand Rapids: Eerdmans, 1993).

2. Thomas C. Oden, op. cit., pp.36, 45.

3. Ibid., p.62.

4. Peter Hinchliff, *Cyprian of Carthage* (London: Geoffrey Chapman, 1974), p.8.

5. Adolf Harnack, *Militia Christi: The Christian Religion and the Military in the First Three Centuries* (Philadelphia: Fortress Press, 1987), especially pp.65-104. For an alternative or at least complementary point of view, see W. H. C. Frend, *The Rise of Christianity* (London: Darton, Longman & Todd, 1984), pp.346-348.

6. Letter 59:6.

7. Peter Hinchliff, op. cit., p.41.

8. Ibid., pp.17-19.

9. Jerome, *De Vir. III*, 53.

10. Maurice Bevenot, art., 'Cyprian, Saint', in *The New Catholic Encyclopedia,* vol 4, p.564.

11. Pontius died c. 260 CE. His *Vita et Passio Cypriani* is the earliest Christian biography.

12. Maurice F. Wiles, 'The Theological Legacy of St Cyprian',

in his *Working Papers in Doctrine* (London: SCM Press, 1976), p.69.

13. *On the Lapsed,* 5.

14. Letter 4.

15. See the classic work of W. H. C. Frend, *Martyrdom and Persecution in the Early Church* (Garden City: Doubleday, 1967).

16. Peter Hinchliff, op. cit., pp.48ff.

17. See the very fine essay of J. Patout Burns, 'On Rebaptism: Social Organisation in the Third Century Church', *Journal of Early Christian Studies,* 1, 1993, pp.367-404.

18. Peter Hinchliff, op. cit., p.100.

19. Ibid., p.102.

20. Hans Von Campenhausen, *Ecclesiastical Authority and Spiritual Power in the Church of the First Three Centuries* (London: A. & C. Black, 1969), pp.272ff.

21. John D. Laurance, *'Priest' as Type of Christ: The Leader of the Eucharist in Salvation History According to Cyprian of Carthage* (New York and Berne: Peter Lang, 1984).

22. Johannes Quasten, *Patrology,* vol. 2 (Westminster, MD: Newman Press, 1953), 381. Citations from Letter 63 are taken from Graeme W. Clark, *The Letters of St Cyprian of Carthage,* vol. 3, Letters 55-66 (New York/Mahwah: Newman Press, 1986).

23. The letter has been described by Batiffol as 'the most notable document on the Eucharist in the Christian literature of the first three centuries', cited in Raymond Johanny, 'Cyprian of Carthage', in Willy Rordorf and others, *The Eucharist of the Early Christians* (New York: Pueblo Publishing Company, 1978), p.156.

24. Graeme W. Clark, op. cit., p.294.

25. Gregory Dix, *The Shape of the Liturgy* (London: Dacre Press, 1945), pp.115f. For a somewhat different reading of Cyprian on eucharistic sacrifice see: Maurice F. Wiles, op.

cit., especially pp.17ff; and Rowan Williams' magisterial response to Hanson in his *Eucharistic Sacrifice, the Roots of a Metaphor* (Bramcote, Notts: Grove Books, 1982). The most developed work on the subject is the above-mentioned work of John D. Laurance.

26. Raymond Johanny, 'Cyprian of Carthage', in Willy Rordorf and others, *The Eucharist of the Early Christians* (New York: Pueblo Publishing Company, 1978), p.174.

27. For a moving, imaginative presentation of the martyrdom of Cyprian, see Peter Hinchliff, op. cit., pp.104.

28. Sebastian P. Brock, 'Syrian Spirituality', in Gordon S. Wakefield, ed., *A Dictionary of Christian Spirituality* (London: SCM Press, 1983), p.367.

29. Peter Robson, 'Ephrem as Poet', in John H. Eaton, ed., *Horizons in Semitic Studies* (Birmingham, UK: University of Birmingham, Department of Theology, 1980), pp.34-35.

30. Sebastian P. Brock, 'The Oriental Fathers', in Ian Hazlett, ed., *Early Christianity: Origins and Evolution to AD 600* (London: SPCK, 1991), p.163.

31. Robert Murray, *Symbols of Church and Kingdom: A Study in Early Syriac Tradition* (Cambridge: Cambridge University Press, 1975), p.31.

32. Sebastian P. Brock, *The Luminous Eye: The Spiritual World Vision of St Ephrem* (Kalamazoo: Cistercian Publications, 1992), p.13.

33. Ephrem, 'Hymn on the Nativity, No. 14', in A. E. Johnston, tr., *Nicene and Post-Nicene Fathers,* second series (Grand Rapids: Eerdmans, 1964), vol. 13, pp.251-252.

34. Ephrem, 'Hymns on Faith, No. 1', in Sebastian P. Brock, tr., *Harp of the Spirit* (Oxford: Fellowship of St Alban and St Sergius, 1975), p.7.

35. Ephrem, 'Hymns on Faith, No. 10', cited in Sebastian P. Brock, *The Luminous Eye,* op. cit., p.104.

36. 'Hymns on Virginity', 16:5, in Kathleen McVey, ed.,

Ephrem the Syrian, Hymns (Mahwah, NJ: Paulist Press, 1989), p.330.

37.   See Samuel Balentine, *The Hidden God: The Hiding of the Face of God in the Old Testament* (Oxford: Oxford University Press, 1983), for a superb analysis of this theme.

38.   'Hymns on the Faith', 8:9, cited in Sebastian P. Brock, *The Luminous Eye,* op. cit., p.27.

39.   'Hymns on the Faith', 51:2-3, in Sebastian P. Brock, *The Luminous Eye,* op. cit., p.28.

40.   Seely J. Beggiani, *Early Syrian Theology* (Lanham, Md: University Press of America, 1983), p.25.

41.   'Hymns on Virginity', 20:2, cited in S. J. Beggiani, op. cit., p.25.

42.   Kathleen McVey, op. cit., pp.10-11. See also Roberta C. Bondi, 'The Spirituality of Syriac-speaking Christians', in Bernard McGinn, John Meyendorff and Jean Leclercq, ed., *Christian Spirituality: Origins to the Twelfth Century* (New York: The Crossroad Publishing Company, 1985), p.159.

43.   'Hymns on the Nativity', 13:7, cited in Kathleen McVey, op. cit., p.138.

44.   Brian McNeil, 'the Spirit and the Church in Syriac Theology', *Irish Theological Quarterly* 49, 1982, p.92.

45.   'Discourse 3', cited in Sebastian P. Brock, *The Luminous Eye,* op. cit., p.99.

46.   Ibid., p.101.

47.   Ibid., p.99.

48.   Ibid., p.100.

49.   Ibid., p.101.

50.   Ibid., p.104.

51.   Ibid., pp.105-106.

52.   Friedrich Von Hugel, *The Mystical Element of Religion,* 2 vols (London: Dent, 1908); *Eternal Life* (Edinburgh: T. & T. Clark, 1912); *Essays and Addresses on the Philosophy of Religion,* 2 vols (London: Dent, 1921).

53. *Essays and Addresses,* vol. 1, op. cit., p.293.

54. Ibid., 264.

55. Friedreich Von Hugel, *Selected Letters,* ed., B. Holland (London: Dent, 1927), p.84.

56. *Eternal Life,* p.365.

57. See David Tracy, 'Freedom, Responsibility, Authority', in P. J. Howell and G. Chamberlain, ed., *Empowering Authority* (Kansas City: Sheed and Ward, 1990), pp.34-47, especially p.41. See also the very fine pastoral application of Von Hugel in Gerard W. Hughes, *God of Surprises* (London: Darton, Longman & Todd, 1985), pp.10-25.

Chapter 2: Medieval Eucharistic Theology

1. Austin Flannery, (ed.), *Vatican II: The Conciliar and Post-Conciliar Documents,* rev. ed. (Northport, NY: Costello Publishing Company, pp.7-8, 1987).

2. Ibid., p.109.

3. Nathan Mitchell, *Cult and Controversy: The Worship of the Eucharist Outside Mass* (New York: The Pueblo Publishing Company, 1982), pp.75-76.

4. Ibid., p.81.

5. Ibid., p.82.

6. Liam Walsh, *The Sacraments of Initiation* (London: Geoffrey Chapman, 1988), p.230.

7. Nathan Mitchell, op. cit., p.137.

8. Liam Walsh, op. cit., p.231.

9. Henry Chadwick, 'Ego Berengarius', *Journal of Theological Studies,* NS 40, 1989, p.416.

10. Nathan Mitchell, op. cit., p.147.

11. Henry Chadwick, op. cit., p.418.

12. Gary Macy, *The Theologies of the Eucharist in the Early Scholastic Period* (Oxford: Clarendon Press, 1984).

Chapter 3: The Reformers and Eucharistic Ecclesiology

1. Edinburgh: T. & T. Clark, 1993.
2. Edinburgh: T. & T. Clark, 1995.
3. References from Luther's works will normally be taken from J. Pelikan and H. T. Lehmann, ed., *Luther's Works*, 55 vols (St Louis, MO: Concordia Publishing House; Philadelphia: Fortress Press, 1955-1986) cited as LW with volume and page number(s).
4. LW 39:68.
5   For example, LW 37:364; 41:154; 40:34.
6. LW 16:32.
7. Eric W. Gritsch, *Martin – God's Court Jester: Luther in Retrospect* (Philadelphia: Fortress Press, 1983) p.187.
8. LW 12:263.
9. LW 35:51
10. Lw 35:53-55.
11. Emphasis added. Heiko A. Obermann, 'Simul Gemitus et Raptus; Luther and Mysticism,' in Steven A. Ozment, ed., *The Reformation in Medieval Perspective* (Chicago: Quadrangle Books, 1971), pp.220-221. See the interesting study of Mihreteab Gebrehiiwet, *Christ Mysticism in the Theology of Martin Luther* (STD Dissertation, the Lutheran School of Theology at Chicago), (Ann Arbor: University Microfilms International, 1977), especially pp.112-148. Many of my citations derive from this excellent study.
12. LW 10:324.
13. LW 26:357.
14. 'The Blessed Sacrament of the Holy and True Body of Christ and the Brotherhoods,; cited in M. Gebrehiiwet, op. cit., p.135.
15. William R. Crockett, *Eucharist: Symbol of Transformation* (New York: The Pueblo Publishing Company, 1989), pp.130ff.

16. David C. Steinmetz, *Luther in Context* (Bloomington: Indiana University Press, 1986), p.72.

17. W. Peter Stephens, *Zwingli: An Introduction to His Thought* (Oxford: The Clarendon Press, 1992), p.95.

18. An English translation of the letter may be found in H. Wayne Pipkin, trans., *Huldrych Zwingli, Writings,* vol. 2 (Allison Park, PA.: Pickwick Publications, 1984), pp.131-144.

19. William R. Crockett, op. cit., p.137.

20. Ibid., p.139.

21. Cited in William R. Crockett, op. cit., p.139.

22. Jacques Courvoisier, *Zwingli, A Reformed Theologian* (Richmond: John Knox Press, 1963), pp.75-77. The liturgy may be found in Bard Thompson, *Liturgies of the Western Church* (Cleveland and New York: The World Publishing Company, 1961), pp.149-155.

23. Ibid., p.154, emphasis added.

24. Jacques Courvoisier, op. cit., p.76. Not all are in agreement with his reading of Zwingli at this point. For an alternative see Brian A. Gerrish, 'Discerning the Body: Sign and Reality in Luther's Controversy with the Swiss in his *Continuing the Reformation: Essays on Modern Religious Thought* (Chicago and London: University of Chicago Press, 1993), pp.66-69.

25. For a similar doctrinal 'transference' in respect of his treatment of the Blessed Virgin Mary, see Walter J. Hollenweger, 'Zwingli's Devotion to Mary', *One in Christ,* 1980/1, pp.59-68, especially pp.66-68. Zwingli's doctrinal hermeneutic, exemplified in Hollenweger's analysis, seems to me to strengthen Courvoisier's reading.

26. This is the theme of Brian A. Gerrish's beautiful book *Grace and Gratitude: The Eucharistic Theology of John Calvin* (Edinburgh: T. & T. Clark, 1993).

27. *Institutes of the Christian Religion,* tr. Ford Lewis Battles (Atlanta: John Knox Press, 1975), 1.2.1.

28. Brian A. Gerrish, *Grace and Gratitude,* op. cit., p.50.

29. Ibid., p.43.

30. *Commentary on the Epistle to the Romans,* 1:9.

31. *Ioannis Calvinis Opera quae supersunt Omnia* (ed. Baum, Cunitz and Reuss; Braunsweig, 1863-1900), vol. 15, 722-725.

32. Brian A. Gerrish, 'Gospel and Eucharist: John Calvin on the Lord's Supper', in his *The Old Protestantism and the New: Essays on the Reformation Heritage* (Chicago and London: University of Chicago Press, 1982), p.109.

33. *Institutes,* 3.1.1; 1.9.1.

34. Ibid., 4.14.6.

35. Brian A. Gerrish, 'Gospel and Eucharist,' pp.110-111.

36. Brian A. Gerrish, *Grace and Gratitude,* op. cit., p.156. See also the earlier but still valuable work of Ronald S. Wallace, *Calvin's Doctrine of the Word and Sacrament* (Edinburgh: Oliver and Boyd, 1953), pp.149-152, 197-216.

37 *Institutes,* 4.17.1.

38. Ibid., 4.17.33.

39. The first three statements are conveniently available in Paul McPartlan, ed., *One in 2000? Towards Catholic-Orthodox Unity: Agreed Statements and Parish Papers* (Slough: St Paul Publications, 1993), and the fourth is published in the *Eastern Churches Journal,* 1, 1993/94, pp.17-25; see also *One in Christ,* 1983/2, 1987/4, and 1994/1.

40. A limited but useful example is available in Lawrence Hull Stokey's book, *Eucharist: Christ's Feast with the Church* (Nashville: Abingdon Press, 1993), especially pp.94-111.

Chapter 4: Pope Pius X to Vatican Council II

1. Thomas Bokenkotter, *Dynamic Catholicism: A Historical Catechism* (New York: Doubleday, 1986), p.218.

2. R. Kevin Seasoltz, *The New Liturgy: A Documentation, 1903-1965* (New York: Herder and Herder, 1966), p.110.

3. Ibid., p.13.

4. Ibid., p.19.

5. Geoffrey W. H. Lampe, ed., *A Patristic Greek Lexicon* (Oxford: Oxford University Press), p.1472.

6. R. Kevin Seasoltz, op. cit., p.21.

7. For example, Linda Gaupin, 'Now Confirmation Needs Its Own Quam Singulari,' in James A. Wilde, ed., *When Should We Confirm?* (Chicago: Liturgy Training Publications, 1989), p.85.

8. R. Kevin Seasoltz, op. cit., p.70.

9. Ibid., pp.91-92.

10. Ibid., p.126.

11. *Mon Univers,* 1924, cited in Henri de Lubac, *Teilhard de Chardin: The Man and His Meaning* (New York: Hawthorne Books, 1967), p.62.

12. R. Kevin Seasoltz, op. cit., p.179.

13. Aidan Nichols, *The Holy Eucharist: From the New Testament To Pope John Paul II* (Dublin: Veritas Publications, 1991), p.102.

14. Anscar Vonier, *A Key to the Doctrine of the Eucharist* (London: Burns and Oates, 1926). The edition cited is from C. J. Dollen, J. K. McGowan, J. J. Megivern, ed., *The Catholic Tradition: Mass and the Sacraments,* vol. 2 (New York: McGrath Publishing, 1979), pp.453-454.

15. Anscar Vonier, op. cit., p.460.

16. Ibid., pp.461.

17. Ibid., pp.471-472.

18. Mark Schoof, *A Survey of Catholic Theology, 1800-1900* (Paramus, NJ: Paulist Newman Press, 1969), p.83.

19. Romano Guardini, *The Spirit of the Liturgy* (London: Sheed and Ward, 1930). The edition from which I quote is from C. J. Dollen, J. K. McGowan, J. J. Megivern, ed., *The Catholic Tradition: Mass and the Sacraments,* vol. 2 (New York: McGrath Publishing, 1979), p.389.

20. Ibid., p.393.

21.   Ibid., p.397.
22.   Ibid., p.403.
23.   Ibid., p.408.
24.   Karl Rahner, *I Remember* (London: SCM Press, 1985), p.74.
25.   Walter Kasper, *Theology and Church* (London: SCM Press, 1985), pp.129-130.
26.   Aidan Nichols, op. cit., p.102.

Chapter 5: Vatican Council II (1962-65)

1.   Robert P. Imbelli, 'Vatican II – Twenty Years Later', *Commonweal* 109, 8 October, 1982, p.78.
2.   Walter Kasper, 'The Continuing Challenge of the Second Vatican Council: The Hermeneutics of the Conciliar Statements', in *Theology and Church* (London: SCM Press, 1989), pp.166-176.
3.   Aidan Kavanagh, 'Liturgy,' in Adrian Hastings, ed., *Modern Catholicism: Vatican II and After* (London: SPCK, 1991), p.68.
4.   Austin Flannery, ed., *Vatican Council II: The Conciliar and Post-Conciliar Documents* (Dublin: Dominican Publications, 1973), pp.4-5.
5.   Ibid. p.16.
6.   Jean Tillard, 'Sacrificial Terminology and the Eucharist', *One in Christ*, 1981/4, p.320.
7.   Austin Flannery, op. cit., p.109.
8.   Ibid., p.110.
9.   Edward Schillebeeckx, *The Eucharist* (London: Sheed and Ward, 1968), p.16.
10.   Ibid., pp.28-29.
11.   Ibid., p.66.
12.   Ibid., p.41.
13.   Ibid., p.69.
14.   Ibid., p.80.
15.   Ibid., p.81.

16.   Ibid., p.98.
17.   Ibid., p.129.
18.   Ibid., p.128.
19.   Ibid., p.131.
20.   Ibid., p.113.

Chapter 6: The Eucharist and Pope John Paul II

1.   Aidan Nichols, *The Holy Eucharist* (Dublin: Veritas Publications, 1991), p.122. Edward J. Kilmartin, *Church, Eucharist and Priesthood: A Theological Commentary on 'The Mystery and Worship of the Most Holy Eucharist'* (Ramsey, NJ: Paulist Press, 1981), p.16.
2.   Edward J. Kilmartin, op. cit., p.15.
3.   Ibid., p.2.
4.   Ibid., p.14.
5.   *Baptism, Eucharist and Ministry* (Geneva: World Council of Churches, 1982) (The Lima Statement).
6.   *Catechism of the Catholic Church* (Dublin: Veritas Publications, 1994).
7.   *Baptism, Eucharist and Ministry*, §1, p.10.
8.   Ibid., §4, p.10.
9.   Ibid., §5, p.11.
10. Ibid., §13, p.12.
11. Ibid., §14, p.13.
12. Ibid., §19-20, p.14.
13. Berard Marthaler, *The Catechism Yesterday and Today: The Evolution of a Genre* (Collegeville: The Liturgical Press, 1995), p.151.
14. Alexander Schmemann, *For the Life of the World* (New York: St Vladimir's Seminary Press, 1963), p.121.
15. For such an approach, but not focusing exclusively on the Eucharist, see the doctoral dissertation of Rowan D. Crews, *The Praise of God and the Problem of Evil: A Doxological Approach to the Problem of Evil and Suffering,*

Ph.D. dissertation (Ann Arbor: University Microfilms International, 1989).

16. Avery Dulles, *The Resilient Church* (Dublin: Gill & Macmillan, 1977), p.181.

Chapter 7: The Eucharistic Presence of Christ

1. Karl Rahner, 'The Presence of Christ in the sacrament of the Lord's Supper', *Theological Investigations*, vol. VI (New York: Crossroad, 1982), p.288.
2. Josef Neuner and Jacques Dupuis, eds., *The Christian Faith* (London: Collins, 1983), p.45.
3. 1 Corinthians 11:20ff.
4. G. W. Clarke, *The Letters of St Cyprian of Carthage*, Vol III (New York: Newman Press, 1986), pp.106-107.
5. Neuner-Dupuis, op. cit., p.414.
6. Karl Rahner, op. cit., p.287.
7. Neuner-Dupuis, op. cit., pp.414-415.
8. See David F. Power, *The Sacrifice We Offer*, Edinburgh: T. & T. Clark, 1987, *passim*.
9. See 1 Corinthians 11:24, and Neuner-Dupuis, op. cit., p.415.
10. Jean Tillard, 'Sacrificial Terminology and Eucharist', in *One In Christ*, 1981/4, pp.306-323.
11. See 1 Corinthians 11:3; Ephesians 5:23.
12. Aidan Nichols, *The Holy Eucharist* (Dublin: Veritas Publications, 1991), p.86.
13. Neuner-Dupuis, op. cit., p.417.
14. Karl Rahner, op. cit., pp.302-303.
15. Thus, Walter Kasper (chief editor), *The Church's Confession Of Faith* (San Francisco: Ignatius Press, 1987), p.288.
16. See the article by Thomas E. Ambrogi in *Lutherans and Catholics in Dialogue* (Minneapolis: Augsburg Publishing Co., 1967), p.157.
17. See Cahal B. Daly, 'Eucharistic Devotion', in Patrick McGoldrick, ed., *Understanding The Eucharist* (Dublin:

Gill & Macmillan, 1969), pp.77-110.

18. Walter Kasper, op. cit., p.286.
19. 'Sacraments', in Robert Morgan, ed., *The Religion of the Incarnation* (Bristol: Bristol Classical Press, 1989), p.158.
20. Walter Kasper, op. cit., p.286.
21. Thomas Ambrogi, op. cit., p.185.
22. Catherine M. LaCugna, *God for us: The Trinity and The Christian Life* (San Francisco: HarperCollins, 1991), p.405.
23. Neuner-Dupuis, op. cit., pp.415f.
24. Karl Rahner, op. cit., p.293.
25. Nicholas Lash, *His Presence In the World* (London: Sheed and Ward, 1968), p.151.
26. Cahal Daly, op. cit., p.88.
27. Ibid., p.101.
28. *Sermon 272.*

Chapter 8: The Eucharist and Social Justice

1. London: Commission for International Justice and Peace, 1980, p.3.
2. A. Flannery, ed., *Vatican Council II: The Conciliar and Postconciliar Documents* (Dublin: Dominican Publications, 1975), p.908.
3. Juan L. Segundo: *The Sacraments Today* (Dublin: Gill & Macmillan, 1980), p.13.
4. New York: Crossroad, 1982, p.10.
5. Enrique Dussell, 'The Bread of the Eucharistic Celebration as a Sign of Justice in the Community', in M. Collins and D. Power, eds., *Can We Always Celebrate the Eucharist?* (Edinburgh: T. & T. Clark, 1982), pp.56ff.
6. 'The Foot Washing (Jn 13:1-20): An Experiment in Hermeneutics', *Catholic Biblical Quarterly* 43, 1981, p.87.
7. Jerome Murphy-O'Connor, 'Eucharist and Community in First Corinthians', in R. Kevin Seasoltz, ed., *Living Bread, Saving Cup* (Collegeville, MN: Liturgical Press, 1982), p.16.

8. These patristic quotations are taken from John McKenna, 'Liturgy: Toward Liberation or Oppression', *Worship* 56, 1982, pp.291-308.

9. Although in respect of eucharistic presence, the Council of Trent was more nuanced than is often appreciated. See chapter 7 above.

10. Austin Flannery, op. cit., p.908.

11. Quoted in Dermot A. Lane, 'Eucharist and Social Justice', in Sean Swayne, ed., *Eucharist for a New World* (Carlow: Irish Institute of Pastoral Liturgy, 1981), p.62. Lane's paper in this collection deserves much wider attention than it has had so far.

12. John McKenna, op. cit., p.294.

13. Johann B. Metz, 'The Future in the Memory of Suffering', *Concilium,* vol. 6, pt. 8, 1972, pp.9-25.

Chapter 9: The Ecumenical Eucharistic Theology of John Macquarrie

1. Enda McDonagh, 'Sacraments and Society', in A. Kee and E. T. Long, *Being and Truth: Essays in Honour of John Macquarrie* (London: SCM Press, 1986), pp.425-436. Geoffrey Wainwright, in his *Doxology,* is one of the few theologians who has given consideration to Macquarrie's theology of worship and the sacraments; see 'Index of persons', s.n. 'Macquarrie, John'.

2. New York: Crossroad, 1997.

3. *Paths in Spirituality* (London: SCM Press, 1972), p.73.

4. *Christian Unity and Christian Diversity* (London: SCM Press, 1975), p.66. In this respect it is helpful to note what Macquarrie has to say about heresy. See his *Thinking About God* (London: SCM Press, 1975), pp.44-51.

5. *Principles of Christian Theology,* revised edition (London: SCM Press, 1977), p.469. Most of Macquarrie's writing on the Eucharist, while it pre-dates the Lima Statement, is

perfectly consistent with the eucharistic theology to be found there.

6. For a general sense of Macquarrie's theology see my 'John Macquarrie, Model of Systematic Theology', in *The Downside Review*, 115, 1997, pp.215-224.

7. *Principles of Christian Theology*, p.470.

8. In his essay, 'Structures for Unity', in Mark Santer, ed., *Their Lord and Ours* (London: SPCK, 1982), p.123.

9. Board for Mission and Unit of the General Synod of the Church of England, *Toward a Church of England Response to BEM and ARCIC* (London: CIO Publishing, 1985).

10. Bishops' Conference of England and Wales, *Response to ARCIC* (London: CTS, 1985).

11. See his 'Eucharistic Agreement?', in John Lawrence, ed., *A Critique of Eucharistic Agreement* (London: SPCK, 1975), p.58.

12. *Jesus Christ in Modern Thought* (London: SCM Press, 1990), p.68. This is also the basis of his treatment, though with a gloss on traditional Anglican positions such as that of Cranmer, in his *A Guide to the Sacraments,* pp.135-145.

13. *The Faith of the People of God* (New York: Charles Scribner's Sons, 1972), p.81.

14. Ibid.; *Principles of Christian Theology*, p.475.

15. Ibid., p.476.

16. Ibid.

17. Ibid., pp.425-426.

18. Ibid., p.426.

19. *Theology, Church and Ministry* (London: SCM Press, 1986), p.176.

20. Ibid., p.178.

21. R. P. C. Hanson provides a fine account of the traditional evangelical Anglican criticism of eucharistic sacrifice in his *Christian Priesthood Examined* (London: Lutterworth, 1979), and, more extensively, in his *Eucharistic Offering in*

the Early Church (Bramcote, Notts.: Grove Books, 1979). Rowan Williams' equally fine reply to Hanson is his *Eucharistic Sacrifice: The Roots of a Metaphor* (Bramcote, Notts: Grove Books, 1982), pp.24-33 are particularly outstanding.

22. *Paths in Spirituality*, p.83.
23. Ibid.
24. *Principles of Christian Theology*, p.474.
25. Ibid., pp.449-450.
26. Ibid., p.477.
27. *Paths in Spirituality*, p.85.
28. Ibid., p.86.
29. Ibid., p.87.
30. *Christian Unity and Christian Diversity*, p.72.
31. William, Temple, *Christus Veritas* (London: Macmillan, 1924).
32. *Paths in Spirituality*, p.88.
33. *Christian Unity and Christian Diversity*, p.72.
34. *Principles of Christian Theology*, p.478; *Paths in Spirituality*, p.88.
35. Ibid., p.88.
36. *Principles of Christian Theology*, p.478; *Paths in Spirituality*, p.88.
37. *Christian Unity and Christian Diversity*, p.75; *Principles of Christian Theology*, p.478.
38. *Christian Unity and Christian Diversity*, p.75.
39. Ibid., pp.75-76.
40. Ibid.
41. Ibid.
42. Ibid., p.88.
43. Ibid.
44. Ibid. Macquarrie is neither explicit nor precise here. Is he referring to the spectrum of 'Protestant' positions in the sixteenth century, or is he referring to contemporary

positions? The context suggests the former, but it is not particularly clear.

45. Ibid.
46. *Principles of Christian Theology*, p.479.
47. *Christian Unity and Christian Diversity*, pp.77-78.
48. Ibid., p.73.
49. See my 'Towards a Post-Liberal Religious Education', *The Living Light*, vol. 28, 1992, and 'Cyril of Jerusalem as a Post-liberal Theologian', *Worship*, vol. 67, 1993.
50. *Principles of Christian Theology*, p.480.
51. Ibid.
52. *Paths in Spirituality*, p.87.
53. F. L. Cross and P. E. More, *Anglicanism* (London: SPCK, 1951), p.464.
54. *Paths in Spirituality*, p.99.
55. Ibid.; *Christian Unity and Christian Diversity*, pp.68-69.
56. Ibid., p.71.
57. *Paths in Spirituality*, p.99.
58. Ibid., see also Nathan Mitchell, *Cult and Controversy: The Worship of the Eucharist Outside the Mass* (New York: Pueblo, 1982), p.417.
59. *Theology Church and Ministry*, p.185.
60. In his *Who's Who in Theology?* (New York: Crossroad, 1992), p.81.

Chapter 10: Liturgy and the Parish

1. Fergus Kerr, 'Liturgy and Impersonality', *New Blackfriars*, 52, 1971, p.436.
2. M. Francis Mannion, 'Agendas for liturgical Reform', *America*, 30 November 1996, pp.15-16.
3. Austin Flannery, ed., *Vatican Council II: The Conciliar and Postconciliar Documents*, rev. ed. (Northport, NY: Costello Publishing Co., 1988), pp.7-8.
4. The translation here of *Sacrosanctum Concilium*, though

entirely accurate and apposite from my point of view, sits somewhat free to the Latin text: '...et ideo in tota actione pastorali, per debitam institutionem, ab animarum pastoribus est sedulo adpetenda.' Cited from Norman P. Tanner, ed., *Decrees of the Eucmenical Councils,* vol. II (London and Washington, DC: Sheed and Ward and Georgetown University Press, 1990), p.824.

5. E. D. Hirsch, *Cultural Literacy* (Boston: Houghton Mifflin, 1987), p.xv.

6. 'The Eucharist, the Church and Evangelisation', *Communio,* vol. 23, no. 4, 1996, p.782.

7. See Owen F. Cummings, 'The Eucharist and Social Justice', *The Clergy Review,* June, 1986.

8. See David Tracy, *The Analogical Imagination* (London: SCM Press, 1981), pp.193-230, 371-390, 405-428.

9. *The Breaking of the Image* (New York: St Martin's Press, 1979), p.82.

10. M. Francis Mannion, 'Catholic Worship and the Dynamics of Congregationalism,' *Chicago Studies* 33, 1994, p.59.

MIC LIBRARY
WITHDRAWN FROM STOCK